MARCO  POLO

VIETNAM

T0166800

Tropic of Cancer

CHINA
Hanoi   Hong Kong

LAOS

South China Sea

**MYANMAR
(BIRMA)**

**THAI-
LAND**

VIETNAM

Bangkok

CAMBODIA

Ho Chi Minh City
(Saigon)

MALAYSIA

www.marco-polo.com

FREE!

THE
TOURING APP

shows you the way...
including routes and offline maps!

GET MORE OUT OF YOUR MARCO POLO GUIDE

IT'S AS SIMPLE AS THIS

1 go.marco-polo.com/viet

2 download and discover

GO!

WORKS OFFLINE!

SYMBOLS

  Insider Tip

★ Highlight

  Best of ...

☼ Scenic view

  Responsible travel: for
ecological or fair trade
aspects

(*) phone numbers that
are not toll-free

**PRICE CATEGORIES
HOTELS**

Expensive 2,600,000 dong

Moderate 1,040,000–
2,600,000 dong

Budget under 1,040,000
dong

The prices are minimum prices
for a double room per night in
one particular hotel

**PRICE CATEGORIES
RESTAURANTS**

Expensive over 260,000
dong

Moderate 130,000–
260,000 dong

Budget under 130,000
dong

The prices are for one meal
per person without drinks

CONTENTS

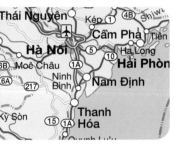

MAPS IN THE GUIDEBOOK
(136 A1) Page numbers and
coordinates refer to the road
atlas
(0) Site/address located off
the map. Coordinates are
also given for places that are
not marked on the road atlas
(U A1) Coordinates for the
map of Saigon inside the
back cover. Map of Hue p. 71,
map of Saigon/Cho Lon p. 93,
map of Hanoi p. 142/143

(📖 A–B 2–3) refers to the
removable pull-out map
(📖 a–b 2–3) refers to the
inset map on the pull-out
map

INSIDE FRONT COVER:
The best Highlights

INSIDE BACK COVER:
Map of Saigon

The best MARCO POLO Insider Tips

Our top 15 Insider Tips

INSIDER TIP **Perspectives in black and white**

Atmospheric and affordable: Long Thanh is one of Vietnam's best photographers. You can buy prints of his remarkable work in his *gallery in Nha Trang* → **p. 31**

INSIDER TIP **Stylish accommodation**

A fantastic breakfast, roof-top pool and the night market around the corner: at the hotel *La Belle Vie* in Hanoi you can enjoy the "beautiful life"! → **p. 48**

INSIDER TIP **Coffee history**

Even those who love tea turn into "coffeeholics" here: the collection of the *Trung Nguyen Coffee Museum* in Buon Ma Thuot reflects the culture of coffee around the world. Fresh coffee is also on offer → **p. 56**

INSIDER TIP **Eat like an emperor**

Immerse in the imperial period: *Truc Lam Vien*, a delightful garden restaurant in Da Nang, serves a wide range of tasty dishes → **p. 62**

INSIDER TIP **Cool rendezvous**

Chilling out, shopping and people watching over eight floors! The *Café Apartments House* is a hotspot in Saigon → **p. 94**

INSIDER TIP **Painted with sand**

So lovely! Artists in Nha Trang, Phan Thiet or Saigon use natural sand in different colours to create decorative *sand paintings* with motifs ranging from Santa Claus to the pope → **p. 30**

INSIDER TIP **Limestone giants**

Hooked on climbing! By rope up-hill, and a descent head first into the water: The *Ha Long Bay* (photo right) and the *Lan Ha Bay* near Cat Ba have become a climbers' paradise in Vietnam → **p. 117**

INSIDER TIP **Sleep in style**

A new chain has brought modern, stylish and friendly hostel accommodation to Saigon. Backpackers are spoilt with well-designed rooms and lots of fresh fruit, for example at *Town House 50* → **p. 87**

BEST OF ...

FOR FREE

● *Hanoi tour with buddies*
A fun tour in Vietnamese: the students of *Hanoi E-Buddies* speak fluent English and are proud to show you their city and its traditions. Participants only pay for admissions and snacks consumed on a culinary street-food tour→ p. 47

● *An early-morning work-out with the locals*
Join the early-bird athletes, who meet up every morning between 5am and 7am by *Lake Hoan Kiem* in Hanoi for aerobics, badminton or a jog around the lake. You don't have to be a tai chi expert! (photo) → p. 43

● *Queuing for Ho Chi Minh*
Tourists are invited to show reverence to the country's revered father figure at Hanoi's *Ho Chi Minh Mausoleum*. After queuing up among Vietnamese people from all over the country, you shuffle respectfully past the glass sarcophagus → p. 43

● *Be a guest of the Jade Emperor*
A ride with the Gods ghost train, please! Admission to the incense-shrouded world of the Taoists and their ruler in the Saigon *Chua Ngoc Hoang* is completely free of charge – for outsiders, it's a confusing array of folk heroes, gods and demons → p. 91

● *Militarily precision – experience the "old" Vietnam*
At 9pm on the dot, and with great military pomp, the Vietnamese flag is lowered on *Ba Dinh Square* in Hanoi. In today's turbo-capitalism it's a nostalgic trip down memory lane, providing a glimpse of the "old" Vietnam with its parade ground discipline without a museum ticket → p. 43

● *The multi-colour world of the Cao Dai sect*
Admission to the main Cao Dai temple in Tay Ninh is not free. But you can visit the *Cao Dai temple* in Da Nang free of charge and even take part in a service – but you'll have to be as quiet as a mouse → p. 61

●●●● Dots in guidebook refer to "Best of..." tips

● *In the footsteps of Confucius*

The *Van Mieu* Temple of Literature in Hanoi is the epitome of Confucian architecture. It was built almost 1,000 years ago in honour of the wise master. A very imposing structure and a must for any visitor to Vietnam → **p. 44**

● *Shake the wok!*

Hoi An without a *cookery course* is like a trip to Vietnam without buying a souvenir straw hat. There is no better place to learn how to prepare spring rolls or a hot pot. For sensory impressions at the market and by the stove, try the Brother's Café → **p. 67**

● *Amphibious action on the Mekong*

Barges full of coconuts and rice, sampans with watchful eyes painted on the bow – the waterways of the Mekong Delta are like a marine motorway with *Cai Rang Floating Market* near Can Tho. The hardest part is knowing where to start → **p. 78**

● *A cyclo adventure*

A tourist on a three-wheeler *cyclo tour* might justifiably feel a little anxious, as the driver cycles straight into the mêlée at a congested crossroads – but as if by divine intervention a gap miraculously appears in the avalanche of sheet metal → **p. 90**

● *Dine like an emperor*

Be like the emperors of yesteryear and enjoy a nine-course *Royal Dinner* in the superb *Ancient Hue* restaurant – with lots of different tastes and in classy surroundings → **p. 72**

● *David versus Goliath*

When you're on your Vietnam trip, don't miss the opportunity to crawl through Saigon's *Cu Chi tunnels*, the underground galleries used by the Vietcong. Afterwards, you will understand a little better how a small, but determined David defeated the giant Goliath with its vast stocks of napalm bombs (photo) → **p. 100**

● *A look into the future*

The Vietnamese like to have their future told. You too can *look into the future:* at one of the hill tribes in Cao Bang or Sa Pa → **p. 36**

BEST OF ...

● *All of Vietnam's ethnic groups at a glance*
The *Museum of Ethnology* in Hanoi provides a fascinating insight into the everyday lives of the many different peoples who make up Vietnam's population – you can even climb inside one of the traditional long houses (photo) → p. 42

● *Smells, crowds and noise*
Shop and eat until midnight in the large *Dong Xuan market hall* in the old quarter of Hanoi. Fresh fish and sweets, lacquerware, T-shirts and ... karaoke! → p. 46

● *An Art Deco gem*
The summer palace *Dinh 3* of Bao Dai, Vietnam's last emperor, in Da Lat is lika a journey back in time on the creaking floorboards of 26 rooms → p. 58

● *Shiva, Ganesha & co.*
The full panoply of the gods: The *Cham Museum* in Da Nang houses an amazing collection documenting the culture of the Hindu Cham, who settled in central and south Vietnam for 800 years: sculptures and delicate reliefs from a lost empire → p. 61

● *Ho, Ho, Ho Chi Minh*
Fascinating – here are the original propaganda posters, but you can also meet school classes and local visitors finding out about the life and work of their country's father and revolutionary: the *Ho Chi Minh Museum* in Saigon → p. 93

● *Shop until you drop*
If you think Vietnam is cheap, then treat yourself to a luxury shopping spree in Saigon. The *Vincom Center* is a shopping mall with many famous designers and fashion brands from all over the world represented – no fakes this time, but expensive imports → p. 96

RAIN

RELAX AND CHILL OUT
Take it easy and spoil yourself

● *For foodies and chocoholics*
Need a break after morning sightseeing in Hanoi? Then check out the seemingly endless *chocolate buffet* in the Le Club café-restaurant in the legendary Sofitel Metropole → **p. 48**

● *Reincarnation with spa treatment*
Jet lagged, stressed out from too much sightseeing or got blistered feet? Whatever you choose, whether it's gentle massaging hands or hot stones, warm chocolate or aromatic essences, after a pamper treatment at *La Maison L'apothiquaire Spa* in Saigon you will feel fully renewed (photo) → **p. 96**

● *Chilling by the fire*
Surprised by the cold winter nights in Sa Pa? Warm yourself up by the fireplace in the cosy *Nature Bar & Grill* with a mulled wine and then choose from a range of hearty game dishes → **p. 52**

● *Cocktails & beach*
Feet buried in the sand sipping a mango margarita in the *Sandals Restaurant beach bar* – now that's how to see out a busy day. The beautiful peninsula of Mui Ne in the south of Vietnam is the perfect setting for some rest and relaxatlon → **p. 86**

● *A literary journey through Vietnam's colonial era*
Take a journey back in time, put Saigon's hurly-burly behind you and browse Graham Greene's classic "The Quiet American" in style where it all happened – under the frangipani trees in the courtyard café of the venerable *Hotel Continental* → **p. 98**

● *Let yourself go*
Simply sit back on the sun deck and take a relaxing *boat tour* along the extensive network of rivers and channels that make up the Mekong Delta – preferably on a converted rice barge → **p. 129**

INTRODUCTION

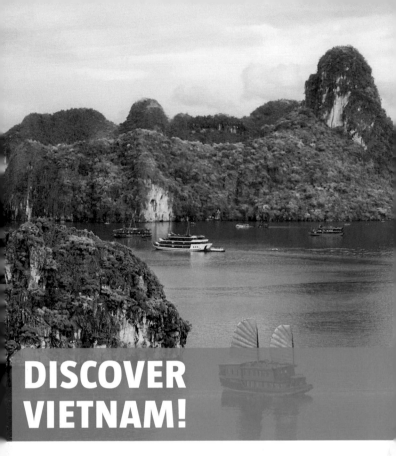

DISCOVER VIETNAM!

"Bonjour, madame." The old monk bows hesitantly, as if in slow motion, at the same time removing the wine-red woolly cap from his bald head. In his wrinkled hand a visiting card bearing the greeting "Happy New Year". Emerging from behind his hunched Methuselah back a Mohican-style tuft of hair. The novice stoops to present a *chom chom*, a hairy, red rambutan fruit. Normally it's the visitors who offer gifts here, not the monks, but no one expects any sacrificial offerings from foreigners – sometimes they rush in and, after a flurry of camera flashlights, quickly disappear; the *Buddhas and the monks* take it all in their stride. Wind chimes tinkle in the breeze that blows through the hallowed halls of the temple. Breathe deep, at last here's somewhere away from the clatter of mopeds and the cacophony of hooting cars, a place to pause, a place for a dialogue with Buddha.

Vietnam is a country moving swiftly into the future. Moss and a patina shroud *monument thousands of years old*, but on the streets of Saigon and Hanoi the modern world is everywhere. A country between past and future, moving away from the clichés associated with the Vietnam War, opium pipes and snake wine. Today's travellers are charmed by the species-rich national parks and *natural*

A blaze of colour to please the gods – temple near the ancient Imperial city of Hue

treasures, from the spectacular Ha Long Bay in the north to the amphibian world of the Mekong Delta in the far south. In between, some *3,200 km/2,000 mi of coastline* dotted with islands, beaches and remote hideaways. In the cities, beside broad, tamarind-shaded avenues, colourful Chinese temples sit comfortably alongside colonial mansions and weather-worn villas in shades of soft ochre. At the same time the skyline rises higher with every blink of the eye. And, mopeds, *mopeds everywhere* – this is most people's first impression of the country. They often just emerge like swarms of bees, laden with boxes full of cola bottles or Tiger beer, bulging shopping bags, chicken cages, and weighed down with two or three children, betel-chewing old men or women in fluttering ao dai gowns and wearing white gloves to protect against the sun and the dirt. Or hot pants like the younger generation.

8th–4th century BC
The Viet migrate from southern China

3rd century BC
The Au Lac kingdom is established in the Red River delta as a bulwark against the Chinese

111 BC–AD 930
North Vietnam is ruled by the Chinese. From the 7th century onwards the Cham kingdom emerges in the south

938
Vietnam gains independence under General Ngo Quyen

1009
First stable dynasty under Ly Thai To. Thang Long (Hanoi) becomes the capital

Vietnam can look back on 4,000 years of history, but few other countries have suffered so painfully from wars and foreign rule by the Chinese, the French, the Japanese and finally the Americans. The same nationalities are returning, but this time they come in peace. Almost 13 million annual visitors – most of them Chinese, Japanese and Russian – and impressive annual growth rates prove it: this south-east Asian country is booming, also as a *travel destination*. Thus, it can become crowded, especially arond Ha Long Bay and in nice resorts such as Mui Ne. Most of the 94 million Vietnamese people moved on long ago from the devastating Vietnam War; half of all inhabitants are under 25 years of age and only know about it from history books. Holidaymakers can now safely give the Ho Chi Minh trail and the Vietcong tunnels a miss – Vietnam has much more to offer. Now travellers can go on journeys of *discovery* wherever they please. It could be to the enchanting pagoda around the corner wafting with scented smoke, the bustling market with fruit sellers and Chinese traders advertising fabrics and pots, idyllic unspoilt beaches or the semi-organised mayhem on the sometimes badly pot-holed roads.

> **Vietnam is a country on the brink of the future**

And then there's this friendly, sometimes mischievous *curiosity*. Wherever there's a *tay*, a Westerner, there's always something happening, something to laugh about. They do well from selling something to the *tay* and, it's true, a few travellers regard

15th–17th century
First European trading posts in the south

1771–1802
Tay Son rebellion. Hue becomes the seat of the Nguyen emperors (until 1945)

1858
Start of French colonial rule

1954
Partition of Vietnam, military rule in the south

1964
Start of the Vietnam War, which the communists win in 1975

1976 (2 July)
The Socialist Republic of Vietnam is founded

their methods as intrusive. But if you don't react to their sales pitch, most *traders* quickly lose interest. Children try out their English and shout "I love you" or "Hello mister!". *Respect for others*, especially one's elders, is considered a virtue; it's a Confucian commandment, together with ancestor worship and hard work. Often up to three generations live in one room, so that could easily be seven or eight people. An apartment, a little house? Unthinkable on *modest wages*. A woman working in a factory will take home £3.50–5.50/US$5–7 a day, if she is prepared to work for up to 14 hours mixing noodle dough, pressing moulds or sorting screws. Living space in Saigon has become unaffordable; the few available plots of land, homes or apartments change hands quickly for the equivalent of many hundreds of thousands of pound sterling or dollars.

> **Important values – hard work, respect and ancestor worship**

Welcome to turbo-capitalism! Doi Moi, the *economic reforms* introduced by the communist government in 1986, has transformed Vietnamese society. Profit is a new word in the Vietnamese vocabulary. The average annual income is estimated at around £1,600/US$2,100. In the last two decades poverty has more than halved, but the urban-rural divide is still great. While the largest ethnic minority, the Chinese, dominate the business world, especially in the cities of southern Vietnam, most of the country's 54 ethnic groups live in the mountains and in the central highlands. These minorities are still in the transitional phase between a life revolving around *ancient traditions and modern life*. Each group wears its own costumes, celebrates its own festivals and follows its own customs.

Vietnam's *scenic beauty* is enchanting. In the tropical southern zones, the pattern is damp, sultry summers and warm winters, whereas in the sub-tropical north the climate is characterised by hot summers, but cooler, wet winters. Many are overwhelmed by *Ha Long Bay* with its towering limestone rocks and darkly shimmering water, but also the breathtakingly rugged "Vietnamese Alps" in the north-west, which can even get a covering of snow in cold winters. There are several terrific Unesco sites in the country, from World Heritage Sites to biosphere reserves. With its "Palace of Supreme Harmony" and imperial tombs, the old *Imperial city of Hue* on the Perfume River is impressive. Near Phan Thiet warm sand crunches underfoot

2000 Trading agreement with the United States. President Bill Clinton visits Vietnam.

2005 Opening of the 6.3 km/ 3.9 mi Hai Van tunnel between Da Nang and Hue

2008/2009 After the economic miracle (from 1991), the world financial crisis hits Vietnam

2010 Hanoi is 1,000 years old – a celebration on 10.10.10 commemorates the event

2011 Vietnam reaches Middle Income Status (US$1,000 per capita) largely as a result of continuing high growth

Vietnam's daily bread – farmers harvesting rice

on the beach at Mui Ne, Saigon with its renovated colonial buildings and a cutting-edge skyline now looks much smarter and in the *Mekong Delta* the chugging engines of the long-tail boats provide an ever-present background beat.

The whole experience is topped off with a wide range of *Vietnamese delicacies* and a perfect holiday schedule of swimming, diving, windsurfing, sailing or hiking in one of the country's 30 or so national parks.

> **Culinary delights and plenty of adventure**

Whether you are hanging upside down from rocks, attempting to climb a limestone pillar in Ha Long Bay, joining in slow-motion tai chi exercises at dawn in Saigon, squinting through the incense smoke of a pagoda or feeling overwhelmed on your bike in the chaotic congestion of Hanoi, eventually you will get closer to the Vietnamese, their ubiquitous dragons and mysterious spirits. There's no question about it – a trip to Vietnam is an *adventure for all the senses*.

2014
Anti-Chinese riots, the conflict between Vietnam and China over the strategically important Spratly and Paracel Islands

2016
The whole of Vietnam grieves for the giant softshell turtle, which lived in Lake Hoan Kiem in Hanoi, and died aged over 100 years

2017
The kidnapping of a Vietnamese, who had applied for asylum in Berlin, hit the headlines. In early 2018, the former politburo member was sentenced to life imprisonment in Hanoi for embezzlement and corruption

WHAT'S HOT

1 Fruitier drinks

Bubbles and beer Forget coffee substitutes and beer brewed only with hops. The latest craze in the fast-living culinary carousel are the brightly coloured *cha,* the bubble teas: you pick the tapioca and jelly pearls yourself, e.g. in the *Koicha (38 Phan Boi Chau)* in Saigon's district 1. Or you can enjoy a pleasant egg coffee in the popular *Café Giang (39 Nguyen Huu Huan | www.giangcafehanoi.com)* in Hanoi's old town. Incidentally, egg coffee was created in the 1940s when there was a milk shortage – it was invented in the luxury Metropol Hotel. The Vietnamese are also famous for their breweries. Usually, light varieties are brewed, but recently in the trendier bars the fashionable local craft beer contains plenty of unusual botanicals: lemon grass, strawberries or mulberries, chocolate brown or chilli hot, sour or smoky – e. g. at *iBiero Craft Beer Station (99 Le Duan | near Lake Hoan Kiem | ibiero.com).*

A break from chaos

Walking streets Pedestrians have right of way in Vietnam! Even if you don't believe it, because of the crazy traffic: the small streets and night markets in the increasingly crowded town centres are (temporarily) designated as "walking streets". In Hanoi, the streets *Hang Ngang, Hang Dao, Hang Duong* and *Dong Xuan* are already pedestrian zones. On weekends (Friday to Sunday) from 5pm or 6pm to 11pm, loud, rattling mopeds and other traffic are already banned. Then, live bands and theatre take over the suddenly silent setting at the night market, and the air is clean to breathe again. In Saigon, *Nguyen Hue Boulevard* is a popular promenade and rendezvous.

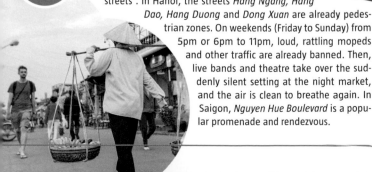

On the beat

Beatboxing It was one day in May 2016. Saigon's city hall was packed with young artists, musicians and students. "I'm a rapper", said Anh, better known by her artist's name Suboi *(photo)*. No lesser than US President Barack Obama was a guest at the relaxed event. He replied: "Go on, let's hear it." The hall applauded. Obama set the rhythm with a burst of beatboxing on the microphone and Suboi started as though she had come straight from New York's Bronx. Beatboxing is a craze for Vietnam's kids. The aim is to perform at popular talent shows, at beatboxing world championships and beatboxing battles. In the "walking streets" (e.g. in Hanoi's old town) and at festivals, the young vocal artists showcase their talent – or every Wednesday in the *Mix & Paint Bar (93 Xa Lo Ha Noi | Thao Dien | Saigon district 2).*

A bird's eye view

Skybars In keeping with the latest trends, the Vietnamese now have their own open air sky bars at dizzying heights. At the ◥ *Chill SaiGon Skybar & Restaurant (AB Tower, 23rd floor | 76 Le Lai | Saigon | www.chillsaigon.com) (photo)* you have to dress to impress! It pays to take advantage of the Happy Hour *(daily 5.30pm–8pm, reservations recommended)*. Or how about a sundowner in the ◥ *Level 23 Wine Bar (Sheraton Tower, 23rd floor | 88 Dong Khoi | Saigon | www.level23saigon.com)* with a sparkling 180-degree panoramic view at night? The open-air bar called ◥ *The Summit (1 Thanh Nien | www.sofitel.com)* on the 20th floor of the Pan Pacific Hanoi (formerly Sofitel Plaza) with its magnificent West Lake view is also an excellent choice.

IN A NUTSHELL

ADVICE FROM THE SPIRIT WORLD

Phuong has had bad headaches for days and doesn't know whether she should accept the office job as an assistant with a foreign company. She kneels with Ms Nguyen before the ancestral altar of her deceased grandfather beneath his large black-and-white photo. As a medium, Ms Nguyen advises in the grandfather's name to put a piece of red paper with Chinese characters under the pillow, so the migraine will disappear. Phuong should also begin the new job the following new year.

Every house in Vietnam has a family altar; no decision about love, illness and careers is made without fortune tellers. The superstition stretches to shamans and feng-shui consultants, miracle healers, elves and spirits and the four mythical animals (dragon, phoenix, tortoise and Qilin, a Chinese mythical and chimerical creature). Taoist superstitions, like unlucky days, lucky years or bad omens, are part of daily reality.

Worshipping the ancestors keeps family ties after death. So that deceased family members don't become restless spirits, at the house altar they must be symbolically given incense and sacrifices like rice, tea, money, cigarettes and alcoholic drinks. In the temples, paper money ("hell money"), paper houses and toy cars are burned.

Nothing should be amiss in the afterlife, not even an Italian designer handbag – made from paper.

Water puppetry and miracles: an old stage tradition is undergoing a revival and the faith in magic spells is flourishing

SPECIAL "DELICACIES"

Welcome to the realm of aphrodisiacs. Superstition is widespread, so Vietnamese men will eat a "virility-enhancing" tiger penis and drink snake wine, eat turtle eggs for a long life or a bird's nest soup. Other "delicacies" include "warming" dog (in the colder north), boiled monkey brains, snake meat, civets, frogs, etc. But don't worry. Such dishes are expensive – the locals would never offer them to an ignorant "long nose", as Europeans are called – plus they should be avoided in order to help protect endangered species.

WHERE SHIVA DANCES

The Hindu god also plays a role in Vietnam, or rather: he dances, if he is not travelling on his bull, Nandi. Those who want to explore the traces of high culture in Vietnam should visit the Cham Museum in Da Nang. Between the 4th and 13th centuries, Champa, the kingdom of their forefathers, was one of the most powerful empires in south-east Asia, extending well into what is now Cambodia. Of the 250 temple sites that once belonged to the Cham civilisation only 20 ruins now remain, one of which is My Son near Da Nang. The architecture and symbolism, such as the lingam, a (phallic) symbol for the Hindu god Shiva, clearly show that the early Cham were Hindus. Their successors of whom about 100,000 are still living in Vietnam, follow the Islamic faith, but it is a very moderate version with its own festivals.

ture reserves are waiting to be explored. The country's last rainforest areas are still a playground for several big cats, including the Indo-Chinese tiger, civet cat and clouded leopard, as well as elephants,

Time for a rest in front of Ho Chi Minh Mausoleum in Saigon

black bears, jackals, skunks, mongoose, flying squirrels, red deer as well as crocodiles and pythons.

Although only about 12 per cent of Vietnam is still covered with tropical forests, they are spectacular, and even zoologists wax lyrical. Who would have thought that in the napalm-scorched and bombed Vietnam so many species would be (re-)discovered – even new species like the antelope-like Saola and muntjac stag, to name just two exotic animals. The most enthralling national parks are Cat Tien, where the last wild elephants roam around and Cuc Phuong with its primate protection project. The biosphere reserves that have the most species are Cat Ba and the remote Phong

IN THE KINGDOM OF THE SINGING GIBBONS

You can leave your heels in the suitcase. In the Vietnamese national parks, hiking shoes and camouflage colours are required – on safari in the ultimate jungle book! For example, when the gibbons tune up for their morning duet choruses. More than 30 national parks and 130 na-

Nha-Ke Bang probably with the world's biggest cave system.

U NCLE HO

Presumably, the country's father would turn in his glass snow-white coffin given all the fuss made about him today with souvenir portraits and propaganda posters. It is well known that Vietnam's former president never wanted to be put on show like in the Ho Chi Minh Mausoleum in Hanoi: "Divide my ashes into three parts and keep them in three ceramic urns that should be the symbol for the north, the centre and the south", he decreed in his will. Even as a young revolutionary Ho Chi Minh fought against French colonial rule, which dated from 1862/63, and in Hong Kong in 1930 he founded the Communist Party of Vietnam. When the country was partitioned in 1954, he became president of the Democratic Republic of Vietnam, usually called North Vietnam. In July 1976, the country was reunited as the Socialist Republic of Vietnam, but it was not an event the still-revered "Uncle Ho" witnessed. He died on 2 September 1969 at the age of 79.

A TOUR ON AN ELE-PHANT'S BACK?

Tourists and elephants in Asia — it's a tricky subject. Be it in Vietnam, Thailand or Cambodia — contact with the domesticated elephants is usually highly commercialised and a lucrative business. Elephant camps are abundant, with a variety of offers from merely interacting with the animals, such as feeding and stroking, to shows with "painting" elephants and ride tours with heavy seats as well as Mahout (trainer) courses lasting several days with the "elephant driver's licence". The line is continually blurred between sanctuary or retirement home for older "jumbos" and enterprising business to entertain tourists. It is advisable to avoid all circus programmes with show artistry that may be unkind for the elephants. A new trend is obvious: the first tour operators are cancelling offers, which include visits to shows, when the elephants provide entertainment. See for yourself how the animals look on the spot, or plan ahead and find out more facts from the local animal welfare organisations.

O N ART AND "ART FAKES"

So many souvenirs — and only one suitcase! But hey, wheely suitcases are mega cheap in Vietnam ... The range of souvenirs is bewildering, and you can find high art, which started with the traditional New Year pictures for the Tet festival — the black-and-white woodcuts known as *tranh tet* — and ceramics produced since the 11th century in villages dedicated to arts and crafts. In the 13th century artists discovered the art of silk painting and set about creating, among other things, portraits used for ancestor worship. The Cham culture with its Buddhist and Hindu figures brought about a revival in sculpture and woodcarving skills. In the 15th century painting with lacquer, a technique which had existed in China for many centuries, became fashionable. Today, hundreds of painters earn a living from copying artworks. Works by Picasso or Rembrandt can be seen hanging on every street corner in Hanoi's Old Quarter, of course, only as inexpensive replicas of the famous masters' oeuvres. You could pick up a Caravaggio or a Dalí up to 1.3 million dong.

N O PAIN ... NO RICE

Did you know? When the Vietnamese talk about food, then they always say "eating rice" – no matter what appears on the table, rice has to be on the menu! It would be hard to imagine the daily routine without rice, a crop the Vietnamese have been growing for thousands of years. Many of the country's myths and legends have grown up around rice. Vietnam is now among the world's top three rice-exporting nations. Some 3 million people in the Mekong Delta alone work as rice farmers. This is where the highest rice yields occur, since the water in the Mekong rises and falls regularly, thus creating optimum conditions for the irrigation of the paddies, which can provide up to three harvests per year.

TOLERANT TOHUBOHU

The first visit to a temple in Vietnam is a minor shock for the uninitiated: it's a confusing and shrill mix of saints in a trumpet-sounding, incense-filled world. The pantheon of the gods is vast; the temples and pagodas are filled with gods and princes of hell alongside mythical heroes and generals, patron saints, demons and dragons. Not one Buddha, but in Mahayana Buddhism at least three Buddhas ensure enlightenment, not forgetting the Bodhisattvas, the sentient beings, foremost among them Quan Am. The Cham brought Hinduism to Vietnam; however, today they practise a rather moderate form of Islam. But religions and philosophies have also intermingled with Christianity: the most bizarre example is the Cao Dai cult, which was founded in 1926, and is a fusion of major religions supplemented by a pinch of the occult, the cult of celebrity and its own pope.

To make the confusion complete: there are still more and more influential guides in daily life and the afterlife. 2,500 years ago Confucius was something like a philosophising lecturer who travelled across China with his ideas and popularised them. For about 1,000 years, Confucianism has also been the prevailing code of conduct within the family and society in Vietnam, and since the 15th century it has even influenced the state structure. The young are subordinate to their elders, women to men, subjects to their ruler. The five most important virtues are "humaneness" (or love), loyalty to one's true nature, reciprocity, filial piety and virtue. In everyday relationships, the oldest male is always the most respected person. So don't be surprised if the first question you are asked is your age!

There is no proof that Lao Tse actually existed; in fact many of his followers see him as a mythical figure, who drew various threads together to define what we now call Taoism. The philosophy emphasises harmony, contemplation and simplicity, as achieved through the Tao or The Way. Key symbols are the Vietnamese equivalents of yin and yang, complementary opposites, unseen (hidden, feminine) and seen (manifest, masculine), with Jade Emperor Ngoc Hoang as the supreme "Ruler of Heaven".

NO MORE WAR!

The Vietnamese prefer not to talk about the past. This mindset corresponds to a degree with the Taoist belief that if you constantly rake over tragic events, in the end you are inviting history to repeat itself. It is important to remember a few facts and figures from eleven years of war, i.e. only from the "American war": an estimated 3.5 million dead (soldiers and civilians, mostly Vietnamese), 600,000 allied soldiers against 200,000 Vietminh fighters from the Communist north and the Vietcong guerrillas. 7.5 million tonnes of bombs dropped from the air (and the same volume on the ground), 80 million tonnes

The Water Puppet Theatre – popular entertainment for more than a thousand years

of agent orange. 10 million refugees and evacuees – nobody knows the exact number of orphans, injured, war invalids and until today stillbirths caused by toxins such as dioxin. But somebody has exactly calculated the costs on the US side: 150 billion US dollars.

Not to mention the devastation of huge swathes of land, villages and towns or terrible massacres such as the one at My Lai. Between 1964 and 1975, the Americans waged an unprecedented war against the forces of the Vietcong. The Cold War, between the US-led western world on one side and Soviet-led communism on the other, was being played out in earnest in this small corner of the globe, with the Vietnamese people being the main victims. Only after the visit to Vietnam by US President Bill Clinton Vietnam, 25 years after the victory of the Vietcong, were relations between the two former adversaries normalised.

LET WATER PUPPETS DANCE

Now, things get wet, colourful, loud and fun: anyone who is afraid of water shouldn't necessarily sit in the front row in the water puppet theatre. Despite Facebook and Twitter, the tradition of *mua roi nuoc,* which is 1,000 years old, is preserved today. It is unique worldwide and was probably developed by rice farmers as a form of entertainment. The puppets, made from fig tree wood, were modelled on villagers, animals, mythical creatures or spirits, they are activated from below the water level with a bamboo stick. They weigh up to 15 kg/33 lbs, so the players need strength and skill, as they also stand in the water behind the curtain. It's still fun, at least for the audience, thanks to the stories from everyday life full of jokes and irony and the figures that whizz through the water.

FOOD & DRINK

Tu Duc, the fourth emperor of the Nguyen dynasty, who ruled the country from Hue between 1847 and 1883, had a passion for fine food. At every meal he wanted 50 dishes, prepared by 50 chefs and served by 50 waiters.

The kitchen staff did their utmost to comply with his wishes... and that's the reason why traditional Vietnamese cuisine alone boasts **over 500 different dishes** today.

All the dishes you order – meat, fish and seafood, eggs, vegetables, salads and soups – are served at the same time, plus of course *com trang (boiled rice)*. On the table will be plates with finely chopped vegetables or fresh herbs, such as basil, coriander, parsley, mint or lemon grass, which can be scattered over

the dishes as required; lettuce leaves are also often included. Also, small but very good *baguettes* are served everywhere, a legacy of Vietnam's French colonial masters. Rice noodles or egg noodles are mainly included in soup (*bun* or *pho*). One variation could be *mien luon*, a **noodle soup** with chunks of eel. Wherever you go, you will find *mien ga,* a noodle soup with chicken, mushrooms, shallots or vegetables. A large bottle of *nuoc mam,* the **fish sauce** made in factories in Phan Thiet and on the island of Phu Quoc, is a standard condiment and should be sprinkled liberally on every dish. The meal opens with the words *xin moi* (please tuck in), whereupon everyone takes their chopsticks to fill their rice bowl and starts eating.

Colourful fresh ingredients and white rice make for delightful dishes that can be balanced between your chopsticks

Restaurant choices range from fine dining to small, roadside food stalls. In upmarket restaurants you will find western-style à la carte menus. In fact, in many hotel restaurants chefs pander too much to the perceived preferences of western diners. Hot flavours are toned down and a lot of fats are used. The many *speciality restaurants* in the major cities and tourist areas, however, are often excellent – proper gourmet eateries serving authentic dishes in a sophisticated ambience.

Because of the cooler climate in the north, the emphasis tends to be more on braised, deep-fried and pan-fried dishes, and also on *rice porridge*. In the emperors' heartlands around Hue, the people eat accordingly: a number of restaurants geared towards tourism there specialise in the dishes once favoured by the Imperial court, so the food is not just splendidly garnished, piquantly seasoned, but also appetisingly presented. If you are in Hue, then you are sure to see *banh khoai* on the menu: crispy pancakes with prawns,

LOCAL SPECIALITIES

Banh cuon – steamed, wafer-thin rice cake with minced meat

Bon bay mon – beef in wafer-thin slices, marinated in various sauces, a Saigon speciality

Bun cha – chargrilled pork patties

Bun thang – hearty soup with rice noodles, chicken and pork, prawns and fried eggs (photo right)

Canh chua – sweet and sour fish soup, heavily seasoned with tamarind, coriander and bean sprouts

Cha – finely sliced marinated pork, chargrilled

Cha ca – finely chopped fish fillets marinated in fish sauce and saffron, threaded on to wooden skewers and grilled

Cha gio – also *nem ran*; spring roll, usually made with thin rice pastry, filled with prawns, pork, egg, noodles and mushrooms, then fried in oil. The transluscent, not fried rolls are called *goi cuon* (photo left)

Com thap cam – fried rice with chicken, pork, sausages, egg yolk, carrots, peas, ginger and other spices

Dua gia – pickled bean sprout salad

Ech tam bot ran – frog meat in batter, fried in oil; served with vinegar, pepper and fish sauce

Ga kho gung – chicken boiled with ginger, fish sauce, sugar and pepper, caramelised (south Vietnam)

Gio – lean pork, crushed in a mortar, then wrapped in banana leaves and boiled

Hot pot – a kind of Vietnamese fondue: fish, seafood, beef, glass noodles cooked in a simmering stock in a samovar or clay pot at the table. Plus onions, tomatoes, mushrooms, beans and other vegetables

Mam chung – fermented fish (from the rice paddy), very aromatic, stuffed and steamed with minced meat, egg, noodles and herbs

pork, bean sprouts and a sauce made from peanuts and sesame seeds. In the south, more exotic, sometimes fiery, ingredients go into the pots and pans. The mixture is stirred briskly, sautéed briefly, grilled and seasoned generously, sometimes with hot spices, e.g. in in *curries*.

But no trip to Vietnam is complete without sampling the fare at one of the wayside *food stalls*. You can usually get a tasty soup or a stew for between 13,000 and 52,000 dong. Outside the main cities look out for restaurants advertising *com pho* (rice soup). Few people speak English in the rural areas, so ask to see the price written down.

Visitors to Vietnam are often advised to get some practice in using *chopsticks*. You can always ask for a knife and fork, but it's much more fun to "do as the Romans do" and that means holding the two sticks delicately between thumb, forefinger and middle finger. Please note: the superstitious Vietnamese believe that chopsticks should never be left standing upright in your bowl. This gesture is used to honour deceased family members. It is impolite to poke around in the food, it's better to just pick out individual morsels. And pointing at people with chopsticks is also considered to be bad manners.

You will find many different kinds of delicious *desserts* in Vietnam. *Banh bao* are a good example. These are small, sweet dumplings filled with meat and vegetables. *Banh deo* are sticky rice cakes soaked in sugar water and filled with fruit and sesame seeds. *Banh it nhan dao,* cakes made from mung bean starch, rice flour and sugar, are steamed in banana leaves. If you fancy candied fruit – it could be fruit or vegetables – then order *mut.* Usually served with Vietnamese tea are sugar-sweet, jellied mung bean cake, known as *banh dau xan,* and as a speciality for Tet, the Vietnamese New Year festival, it has to be *banh chung,* sticky rice cakes filled with beans and meat.

The *fruit selection* is seemingly endless. Incidentally, you will often see fruit used as sacrificial offerings in temples, but each one has a particular symbolism: a coconut, for example, stands for frugality, a papaya for pleasure, a cherimoya fulfils a wish, plums are for longevity, the dragon fruit gives strength, and the "eyes of the dragon" *(longans,* similar to *lychees)* are said to have a relaxing effect. Quench your thirst with mineral water

(nuoc soi) or all kinds of colas and soft drinks. But do not overlook drinks such as the ubiquitous *green tea (che),* fresh coconut milk *(nuoc dua)* or the tasty tropical fruit juices *(sinh to)*. Rice wine may not be to everyone's taste, but few people could dislike the *beer* – either as a *bia*

Chopsticks at the ready? Here, there is plenty of delicious street food

hoi (draft beer) or as Castel, Huda (from Hue), Saigon Export, Bia Hanoi, Salida or 333 (say *ba ba ba*) – and at 13,000–26,000 dong a glass very affordable, in a *bia hoi* corner pub, open air or on a stool for even less.

Vietnamese *coffee* is very good and very strong. When coffee is served, placed on top of the cup will be a special metal filter and ground coffee. Boiling water is then poured on to the coffee, which drains through into the cup containing a generous quantity of condensed milk.

SHOPPING

Vietnam is heaven for souvenir hunters. The shops will have no price tags – you will have to negotiate a price, and you could come away with a bargain. There are lots of antiques, but sellers can often conveniently "forget" that tourists need an export licence. Without this permit, the goods will be confiscated when you pass through customs – even imitation antiques. And caution: jewels are often cheap fakes.

ARTS AND CRAFTS

Silk, hand-painted or printed cotton fabrics, embroidery, copper and silver objets d'art, jewellery, statues, wood carvings, miniatures, leather goods, carpets and beautiful furniture with inlays are available at reasonable prices. Between Hanoi and Ha Long City, there's the *Hong Ngoc Humanity Center (on the N 18 | Sao Do | Hai Duong)*. The goods on sale here include shoes, silk garments, tea sets, books and paintings. How about a statue of Ho Chi Minh in white marble for the terrace at home? At the foot of the Marble Mountains in the village of Quang Nam, master sculptors are kept hard at work – you can hear the hammering of chisels from up in the mountains. **INSIDER TIP** Sand paintings *(tranh cat)* make for quite decorative souvenirs. In Nha Trang, the *Hong Chau Sa family (4b Nha Tho | in the Hong Chong Club House, more shops: 81 Tran Quang Khai, 6 Cau Da and at the Po Nagar temple)* sell works of art depicting everything from landscapes to Santa Claus. The colourful sand comes from Phan Thiet, where you will also find *Phi Long Sandpainting (Alley 4444 | Thu Khoa Hoan | Than-Hai District)*. The most famous artists do portraits on request, such as Marilyn Monroe or the pope, for example in Saigon at *Kim Sa*, *Sand Painting My Art (www.tranhcatmyart.com)* and *Y Lan (www.tranhcatylan.com.vn)*.

CLOTHING

In the silk shops, such as those in "tailor town", Hoi An, you can have practically anything made to measure and in your choice of fabric, all at very affordable prices. If you would like an *ao dai*, the national dress for Vietnamese women, you can get a nice one for around 750,000 dong, but do bear in mind that these silk garments are really intended for warmer climate zones.

Elaborately-decorated straw hats, fine laquerware and tailor-made silk garments – you will find some great gifts in Vietnam

CONICAL HATS

The conical hats are worn by the rice farmers as protection against rain or sun. Good quality hats have thin scraps of paper between the straws. The finest cone hats come from the Hue region. In the hatter's village Phu Cam (also Phuoc Vinh) on the south bank of An Cuu River, the women produce semi-translucent hats made from palm leaves, which they decorate with silk thread, images of the landscape or lines of poetry (also available in the Dong Ba market in Hue).

LACQUERWARE

The resin of the son tree is collected and made into a brown or black lacquer, which is used to decorate accessories and home ware, anything from a tea set to lounge suites. For a more expensive piece in a specialist store, ask how many paint layers were applied. The more layers, the more valuable the item. Ten is the minimum number, the maximum could be 200.

PHOTOGRAPHS

One of the best Vietnamese photographers is Long Thanh. You can buy his pictures in poster format at his INSIDER TIP *gallery in Nha Trang (126 Hoang Van Thu | Nha Trang | www.long than hart.com)*, evocative studies of everyday life with a remarkable, sometimes disturbing interplay between light and shade.

POP MUSIC

The range of cheap CDs is huge. Fusion is the current fad. Huong Thanh ("Dragonfly") is a popular exponent of the gentler version; Vietnam's most popular singer, Than Lam, produces a much more powerful sound. Jazz guitarist Nguyen Le is also renowned for his western-inspired, traditional music. Ethno-jazz performer Billy Bang ("The Aftermath") has a devoted following.

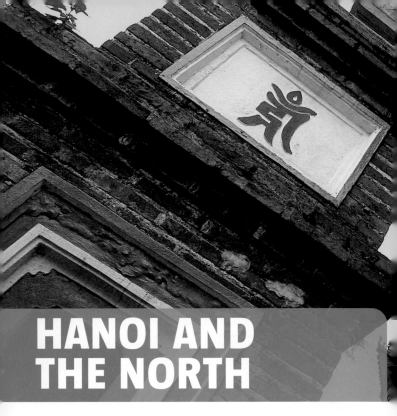

HANOI AND THE NORTH

Uncle Ho overtakes Miss Saigon: for a long time the formerly Communist Hanoi was regarded as the quieter of the two major rural cities, but those days are over.

There is no holding Hanoi back now; the building boom is even threatening the picturesque houses in the old quarter. But the enchanting parks, idyllic lakes and the still quiet corners of the town more than make up for that.

The north is also full of natural wonders: south-east of Hanoi, about three hours away by car, the white limestone rocks of Ha Long Bay, which are overgrown like a jungle, jut out of the water. And the mountain village of Sa Pa is developing rapidly, although it's a long trek by train or bus to see the hill tribes in the north-

west and to explore the landscape with its photogenic rice terraces. Ba Be National Park, a tropical rain forest, is well worth a visit and still undiscovered.

CAO BANG

(137 E1) (⟦ E1) Nestling between two rivers and high, craggy mountains, the capital of one of the most forested Vietnam provinces welcomes its visitors.

The small city (pop. 50,000) is a rather typical, arid border town, but the surroundings are the epitome of green. The region is renowned for its magnificent and wildly overgrown karst hills, free-flowing rivers and rain forests. As a whole day is needed to cover the more

Parks, pagodas and new buildings dominate the capital; mountains and the Red River delta define the surrounding area

than 270 km/168 mi from Hanoi, the little spot makes a INSIDER TIP good starting point for excursions to the impressive 53 m/173.9 ft high and 300 m/984 ft wide *Ban Doc Waterfall* (also known as Ban Gioc waterfall), to the *Ba Be National Park*, the picturesque *Thang Hen Lakes* (four-wheel drive required), *Pac Bo Cave* and the markets of the hill tribes. The town and province is populated mainly by the Tay (Tho), but also by many Nung and some Hmong, where you can sleep in homestays.

FOOD & DRINK

Get a quick meal: there are a number of good, inexpensive food stalls in the market in *Hoang Nhu.*

PIZZA CHI

Who would have thought that sumptuous, yet crispy wood-fired pizza is served up in the mountains of North Vietnam? Don't be deterred by the simple, tube-shaped look of the place! *81 Vuon Cam | mobile 0169 3 80 41 06 | Budget*

Poshness with pineapples: women from the Tay hill tribe carrying heavy loads

SHOPPING

With a little luck, you can buy finely woven, brightly-coloured carpets made by the Tay and Muong minorities on the market. The carvings here are also of a very high quality. Colourful, with very friendly traders and live stock market including water buffalos: the large hill tribe market in *Tra Linh* on the N 3, held on the 4th, 9th, 14th, 19th, 24th and 29th day of the lunar month, is impressing.

WHERE TO STAY

DUC TRUNG ⚏
Pretty, wide view (the higher, the better): this modern hotel offering quiet but bright rooms on six floors with parquet floor, partly with panoramic windows. Near the market and the bus terminal. *24 rooms | 85 Be Van Dan | tel. 0206 3 85 34 24 | duc trunghotel.com.vn | Budget*

THANH LOAN HOTEL
Mesmerising wood carvings: located near the Bang Giang River, the hotel boasts simple rooms, some with balconies, some with a wall view (but quieter than overlooking the street). The wood panelling in the lobby is impressive and the heavy furniture (what does such a grand bed weigh ...?). *32 rooms | 131 Vuon Cam | tel. 0206 3 85 70 26 | Budget*

INFORMATION

Information for tourists can be found in the hotels. If booking excursions, guides and four-wheel drive vehicles, you must call a few days before your arrival.

WHERE TO GO

INSIDER TIP ▶ BA BE NATIONAL PARK
(137 D2) (⟁ E2)
Now for the enchanted fairy tale – and above all tranquillity and solitude: the gigantic limestone mountains on the country's largest lake protrude almost vertically out of the water. It's not surprising that the area is also called the "Ha Long Bay of the Mountains". This lake area about 85 km/52.8 miles south-west of Cao Bang

is over 8 km/5 mi in length, with many islands and valleys in-between with green rice fields. The surrounding mountains over 1,500 m/4,921 ft high make the landscape scenery perfect. In the surrounding tropical rainforest about 300 animal species thrive, including threatened species like the lutung – species diversity here is incredible. A memorable experience is a boat trip through the nearly 30 m/98.4 ft high, 300 m/984 ft long *Puong Cave*. It is home to countless bats, and the rocks and stalactites look eerie in torchlight.

Accommodation near the lakes: *Ba Be Hotel (25 rooms | in the Tay village of Cho Ra 18 km/11.2 mi away | tel. 0209 3 87 61 15 | Budget)* with acceptable rooms and *Mr. Linh's Homestay (14 rooms | in the village of Bo Lu | mobile 098 6 01 60 68 | www. mrlinhhomestay.com | Budget)*. Three-day tours cost around 4,700,000 dong per person *(based on two people, e.g. with Asiatica Travel | www.asiatica-travel. com)*; the price depends on the number of participants and the agency. The cheapest tours are offered in the traveller cafés in Hanoi. A charge of around 26,000 dong is payable in the Visitor Center by the park gates. *National park office: tel. 0209 3 89 41 26*

HA LONG BAY

(137 E–F3) *(ⓜ F3)* **A night by the legendary** ⭐ **Ha Long Bay: on the horizon, a caravan of hunchbacked elephants seems to move past the anchored junk and tourist boats; slightly closer silent guards stand watch in the pale moonlight.**

The swirling mists in the winter months can certainly fire the imagination! About 2,000 islands emerge in all forms and sizes from the waters of the Gulf of Tonkin. There are two possible explanations for their creation. Firstly, a scientific one, which suggests that the rocks were part of the south-western Chinese limestone plateau, which was flooded by the sea after the last Ice Age. And

⭐ **Ha Long Bay**
Simply outstanding – limestone pinnacles emerging from the sea → p. 35

⭐ **Old Hanoi**
Picturesque artisans' houses and bustling street markets → p. 41

⭐ **Ho Hoan Kiem**
This idyllic city lake in Hanoi is not just a lovers' rendez-vous → p. 43

⭐ **Van Mieu**
Confucian simplicity, but of impressive proportions, the Temple of Literature in Hanoi → p. 44

⭐ **Chua Thay and Chua Tay Phuong**
These two Buddhist pagodas are among Vietnam's crown jewels → p. 48

⭐ **Huong Tich Son**
A magnificent karst landscape and the Chua Huong pilgrims' pagoda → p. 49

⭐ **Ha Long Bay on land**
Impressive karst outcrops near Ninh Binh – rocks as far as the eye can see → p. 50

⭐ **Sa Pa**
Get close to the colourfully-dressed hill tribes in the rugged mountains of the north-west → p. 51

MARCO POLO HIGHLIGHTS

then a legend – one of many: to fend off Mongol calvary, a dragon flew down from the sky and destroyed the landscape with its flailing tail. The dragon then dived into the sea, so the water would flood the valley.

What used to be the two idyllic fishing ports of *Hon Gai* and *Bai Chay* are now called *Ha Long City* and are connected by a bridge. They have merged to become one large and lively playground – with an ever-expanding skyline of hotels, a night market, a casino, an overpriced water puppet theatre and a giant circus arena and *Paradise Marina* on the *Tuan Chau Peninsula* 5 km/3.1 mi away.

LOW BUDGET

● Fortune tellers among the hill tribes in Cao Bang or Sa Pa will tell you your fate, for only 26,000 dong. A village shaman will perform fireside rituals using stones and bamboo poles as a "phone" to contact ancestors and spirits.

Everything is just right at the ☆ *Thai Bao Hotel (50 rooms | 1/4 St No. 207 | Promenade | Cat Ba | mobile 097 5 51 47 24 | www.thaibaohotel.com | from 256,000 dong)* near the pier. The owners Vic and Tom offer plenty of tips to go with the great rooms with balconies (Sat-TV, air conditioning, WiFi).

It's even cheaper on Cat Ba – you can camp on the beach and on *Monkey Island (approx. 100,000 to 260,000 dong per tent, mattress and lighting included, but you will have to bring most of your own food)*.

SIGHTSEEING

CAVES

The attraction of Ha Long Bay lies primarily in the countless dripstone caves that can be explored as part of a boat tour. The *Hang Dau Go* or the Cave of Wooden Stakes is so named, because during the 13th century it was used as a hiding place for a large collection of sharp bamboo poles, which the northern Vietnamese people used to put 500,000 Mongols under Kublai Khan to flight. The cave is reached via 90 steps. Do try to visit the *Hang Trong*, the Drum Cave. Wind and weather cause the dripstones to emit noises, said to resemble distant drumbeats. The finest cave of all is the strikingly illuminated *Hang Sung Sot*. The tour groups are dispersed around the three vast chambers; this way they can enjoy the circular tour with its almost mystical vistas in relative peace. Boat tours start in Bai Chay, Hon Gai, Tuan Chau or from Cat Ba Island. *Admission per cave approx. 26,000 dong*

FLOATING VILLAGES

What amazing amphibian activity! In Ha Long Bay, which is about twice the size of Berlin measuring 579 mi^2, more than 1,600 people still live on and from the water. There are only four settlements, including the largest floating villages in Asia, which are hidden between the distinctive limestone islands, like *Cua Van* near Cat Ba. This is a spectacular living place – apart from the expensive electricity for diesel generators and the storms during the typhoon season. Then, the house boats, pontoons and wooden living huts are tied together and chug to a bay offering more protection. The residents in Cua Van, *Van Gia* or *Vong Vieng* mainly earn their livelihood from breeding fish: the floundering "sub-tenants" live directly beneath their houses. Or brightly lit fishing boats attract squid at night. Not forgetting that pearl breeding also depends on floating farms. The village shop is also a floating motor boat with a wooden canopy and even the doctor arrives in a rowing boat. The mayor's house and school are all floating. The villages are on the excursion schedules of many Ha Long tour operators, e.g. *Paradise Cruises (Thuan Chai | www.paradise cruise.com)*.

FOOD & DRINK

HONG HANH

Here, you should be happy if you get a table – the locals know where you can find a good and reasonably priced meal: Choose your own fish or lobster from the tanks with the waitress and know that your food is nothing but fresh. *442 Nguyen Van Cu | tel. 0203 3 83 58 92; branch: 50 Ha Long | tel. 0203 3 81 23 45 | both in Bai Chay | Moderate*

SHOPPING

NIGHT MARKET IN BAI CHAY

There's something going on here every night – piled high on the tables between the promenade and beach are chopsticks, swimwear, shoes, toys and knickknacks of all kinds. And there's a small funfair for children. *Daily 6pm–11pm*

SPORTS & ACTIVITIES

BOAT TOURS

For trips out on to Ha Long Bay and to Cat Ba Island, go to the tourist pier in Bai Chay (near the Thang Long Hotel) for tickets and boats *(from approx. 1,300,000 dong/per boat per day, additional admission approx. 160,000 dong, plus accommodation fee of approx. 210,000–390,000 dong for 1–3 nights)*. Starting in Hanoi, there are three-day trips with accommodation from 1.6 million dong (from about 12 people, often also including a party ...). Waiting for

Magic world of stone: light show in Hang Sung Sot Cave

passengers to arrive are some 400 or so boats, junks and paddle steamers. Ha Long tours also leave from Cat Ba.

to chat over fruit juices, beer, whisky, ice cream and snacks. *Ha Long Road (promenade) | Bai Chay | Budget*

Corner shop on the water: a food trader in the Ha Long Bay

Because now all boats can anchor in one bay, you have to be prepared for plenty of diesel fumes and karaoke-style speaker systems.

KAYAKING

If you want to do more than just swash around the bay, you can explore some of the caves by taking a kayak through a narrow opening and then paddling into the emerald green lagoon, e.g. into the *Hang Luon Cave*. Or you can make a detour to the "floating" fishing villages, such as *Van Gia*.

ENTERTAINMENT

TRUNG NGUYEN 2

It's impossible to overlook or ignore this bar above the main road. A popular place

WHERE TO STAY

BAI THO JUNK/VICTORY JUNK

The floating Ha Long Bay hotel is a good bet: the rooms on the *Bai Tho Junk* or the *Victory Junk* from Victory Star Cruises are well-outfitted with amenities such as whirlpool bath tubs and small balconies. Cookery courses and massages are also offered. *Tel. 0203 3 82 68 98 | mobile (hotline) 091 4 50 35 03 | www.victory halong.com/vn | Expensive*

LA PAZ RESORT TUAN CHAU ☆

The villas and rooms, perhaps in need of renovation, are situated by a private beach or by a hill (large baths, some with jacuzzi) with an amazing panoramic view. Pool, massages, fitness suite, golf course, helicopter flights over the bay. *247 rooms | Tuan Chau | tel. 0203 3 84 29 99 | www.lapazresorts.com | Moderate–Expensive*

INFORMATION

Tourist Service Center (Bai Chay Pier | Ha Long City | tel. 0203 3 84 74 81 | www. halongbay.com.vn)

WHERE TO GO

BAI TU LONG BAY (137 F3) *(ⒶⒶ F–G3)*

Apart from the endless trail of boats: this northern bay is much quieter than Ha Long Bay. There are not so many spectacular caves, but instead you will find several largish beaches, such as on the islands of *Quan Lan* and *Van Don*. King prawns and fish are farmed on Quan Lan and you can still witness some of the surviving traditions, such as the boat races that form part of the village festival in the summer. But as you walk the streets and explore the main village, you will see men at work sawing and hammering. Once the first bungalows are finished, there are bound to be more – on both islands' beaches. Several ferries per day ply between Cam Pha/Cai Rong on the mainland and Quan Lan; they also leave from Hon Gai (Ha Long City). You will find a number of places to stay on the island, e.g. the *Min Chau Beach Resort (50 rooms | Minh Chau Beach | tel. 0203 3 87 78 86 | mobile 090 4 08 18 68 | www.minhchauresort.vn | Moderate)*, a modern hotel near the beach with decent rooms and suites (if a little overpriced), mini-pool, roof bar. If all you need is a bed for the night, you could try the *Robinson huts (Budget)*, but the cabins are rather spartan. Better accommodation is to be found in the town, e.g. the four-storey *Ann Hotel (tel. 0203 3 87 78 89 | mobile 0913 07 20 72 | www.ann hotel.com.vn | Budget)* with 26 nice balcony rooms and large bathrooms.

The island of Van Don further north is connected to the mainland by a bridge. There are two ferries a day from Quan Lan or you can catch the hydrofoil from Ha Long City. At *Bai Dai Beach* at the eastern end of Van Don, it's still quite rural, but you can't miss all the new building work taking place along this part of the coast. An endless stream of freighters, boats and ferries ply across the bay against the magnificent backdrop of rocky islets. In fact, Van Don was a fishing port already 1,000 years ago.

CAT BA (137 E3) *(ⒶⒶ F3)*

Ready for another island? Cat Ba is the largest island in Ha Long Bay and lies some 20 km/12.4 mi south-west of Ha Long City. Especially in the main town, *Cat Ba*, mini-hotels abound, as at weekends it is the preferred destination for countless trippers, seeking the pleasures of the karaoke bars. However, a large part of the island has been designated as a conservation area, so there are limits on how far the tourist developments can go. Wooded slopes extending to a height of 300 m/984 ft, deep gorges, caves and grottoes, as well as beaches enclosed by rocks form a small, Polynesian-style area, a perfect habitat for monkeys and bird species. The best time of year for swimming in the sea is from June to October, at other times it is often cool and misty. If you join a tour of the National Park, you can visit caves, where stone implements and human bones thought to be up to 7,000 years old were found (admission approx. 40,000 dong).

Tapas and pasta, soups and salads, vegetarian fare and seafood is served in the *Green Mango (near the Holiday View Hotel | tel. 0225 3 88 71 51 | Moderate)*. Chic ambience by the promenade.

Alternatively try *The Good Bar (1/4 Street No. 4 | promenade | tel. 0225 3 88 83 63 | Budget)* where climbers meet over pizzas, hamburgers and Vietnamese dishes, plus pool, table football and darts.

Beside a small bay lies the villa-style *Sunrise Resort (39 rooms | Cat Co 3 Beach | tel. 0225 3 88 73 60 | www.catba sunriseresort.com | Moderate–Expensive)* with nice rooms (some with jacuzzi), pool, three restaurants and water sports. Appealing rooms with great views and WiFi can be booked at the ✳ *Sea Pearl Cat Ba (85 rooms | 1/4 Street no. 219 | promenade | tel. 0225 3 69 61 28 | www.seapearlcatbahotel.com. vn | Moderate)* with its rooftop restaurant and a disco on the 1st floor; you can often bargain for a good deal.

HAI PHONG (137 E3) *(ᗰ F3)*

Vietnam's third largest city (pop. 900,000) has kept its colonial charm in some quarters: this is down to the French who from 1876 advanced the port's reconstruction here about 100 km/62 mi south-east of Hanoi. Today, in the *Quartier Français* you can see the delightful architectural gems from the period around 1900 such as the theatre, observatory, city museum, station and post office. Around Dien Bien Phu you will find villas, small mansions, hotels and colonnades. Adjoining to the east is the Old Town. In the pretty, 18th-century *Den Nghe* temple *(corner of Le Chan/Me Linh)* you can see a richly ornamented stone altar; the gilded palanquins date from the 19th century, as do all the furnishings.

The welcoming *Saigon Café (107 Dien Bien Phu | tel. 0225 3 82 21 95 | Moderate)* is a meeting place for travellers from all over the world (often Western-style pop and rock music in the evenings). The hotel *Avani Hai Phong Harbour View (127 rooms | 12 Tran Phu | tel. 0225 3 82 78 27 | www.avanihotels.com | Expensive)* with its elegant colonial style comes well-recommended. It also organizes lots of excursions. The modern *Nam Cuong Hai Phong Hotel (78 rooms | 47 Lach Tray | tel. 0225 3 82 85 55 | www. namcuonghaiphonghotel.com.vn | Moderate)* is not only a good place to spend the night – you can also try the two excellent restaurants and the two pools.

Several times a day ferries leave from *Ben Binh terminal* to Cat Ba island (slow boat 2 hrs, hydrofoil approx. 30 minutes). *Information: Hai Phong Tourism (18 Minh Kai | tel. 0225 3 82 26 16 | www.haiphongtourism.gov.vn)*

HANOI

MAP ON PAGE 142–143
(137 D3) *(ᗰ E3)* **In Hanoi (pop. 3.5 million), you encounter all of them: one of Asia's most beautiful and oldest cities presents a virtual "Who's who" of Vietnamese history.**

Heroes from Confucius to Ho Chi Minh or even modern icons in fast-paced turbo capitalism – including the property boom and traffic chaos.

Spacious parks and about 600 temples, pagodas and magnificent buildings from the European colonial era shape the face of this city, which was founded in 1010, but not named *Ha Noi* or the "city on the bend of the river" until the days of Emperor Minh Mang (1820–41). After the economic boom reached the north of Vietnam, this vast metropolis got moving. Mopeds roar through the streets, the noise of construction work is ever-present, housing and office blocks are springing up everywhere, and today, as in the past, the High Society is staying in the luxury hotels.

SIGHTSEEING

OLD HANOI ★
(142–143 C–D 2–3) *(🗺 0)*

No visitor could possibly ignore Hanoi's Old Quarter. The artisans' district, which was first settled in the 11th century, when Emperor Ly Thai To moved the capital to Thang Long, is a fascinating sight. The "36 streets" from that time have survived the centuries. Each street is named after the goods that were once sold there: *Hang Ca* is Fish Lane, *Hang Bo* Basket Street, *Hang Buom* Sailmakers' Alley, *Hang Non* for hatters and *Hang Hom* for the carpenters who made coffins. Unfortunately, the brick houses from the 19th century are threatened by the construction boom. Even the shop displays have adapted to meet the requirements of the throngs of tourists.

From 3pm, but at its height from 5pm to 9pm in the rush hour, fuming two-wheel

🏙 WHERE TO START?
Start your tour of the city with a walk round **Lake Hoan Kiem (143 D3–4)** *(🗺 0)* from the French (hotel) quarter at the southern end of the lake and then on past the "gymnasts" (early morning and evening), passing the Jade Mountain Temple (Den Ngoc Son) and then on into the heart of Old Quarter. If you're a long way from the starting point, take the *Electric Car Tour*, e.g. from the Water Puppet Theatre or the Dong Xuan market. Or you can take a moped taxi or bus there, nos. 1, 3, 7 or 14.

chaos reigns in the Old Quarter. It's sometimes almost impossible to move, either because the narrow pavements are overflowing with parked mopeds or

Booming trade and traditional life come face to face in Hanoi's Old Quarter

the congested streets are crammed with hundreds of mopeds revving and hooting. If there's room, they simply ride on the pavement – at breakneck speed. The best solution is to just disappear into one of the smart cafés for a tea or find an air-conditioned bar for a *bia hoi* beer. Or, you can come on weekends when the small streets around the Dong Xuan are transformed from Friday to Sunday afternoon into relaxing pedestrian zones.

The red Huc bridge crosses to the Den Ngoc Son Temple

CHUA MOT COT (142 A2) *(ⴰ 0)*

There's a charming legend behind the "One Pillar Pagoda". One night the goddess Quan Am appeared before the ageing and childless emperor, Ly Thai To, and presented him with a baby boy. There was now a male heir in the royal family and so, out of gratitude to the goddess, Ly Thai To built a stone pillar as a memorial shrine in the form of a lotus flower. In 1954 the column was destroyed

by the French, but a concrete replica was built as a replacement. Quan Am is still revered as a symbol of fertility. *Daily sunrise to sunset | on Chua Mot Cot street, south of the Ho Chi Minh Mausoleum*

CHUA QUAN SU (142 C4) *(ⴰ 0)*

The "Ambassadors' Pagoda" is always a hive of activity, but then it is the city's Buddhist centre. During the 15th century the building was used as a hostel for Buddhist emissaries from other countries. *Daily approx. 6am–9pm | 73 Quan Su*

DEN NGOC SON (143 D3) *(ⴰ 0)*

The "Jade Mountain Temple", which stands on an island in the northern Lake Hoan Kiem is dedicated to three individuals: General Tran Hung Dao, who defeated the Mongols during the 13th century, the scholar Van Xuong, and La Tho, the patron saint of physicians. You can reach the temple via the pretty The Huc bridge (Bridge of the Rising Sun). *Daily 7am–6pm, during winter 7.30am–5.30pm | admission approx. 26,000 dong*

DEN TRAN VU (142 B1) *(ⴰ 0)*

The Tran Vu Temple (also Quan Thanh), the most important Taoist temple in Hanoi, was built in 1010 outside the city gates. It is dedicated to the demon and sorcerer, Huyen Thien Tran Vu. He was revered outside the central zone, so as to spare the city itself any misfortune. The 4 m/13.1 ft high bronze version of Tran Vu, weighing nearly 4 t, dates from 1677. *Daily 8am–6pm | admission approx. 13,000 dong | Quan Thanh, on the southeastern shore of the West Lake*

INSIDER TIP▶ MUSEUM OF ETHNOLOGY ● (0) *(ⴰ 0)*

54 ethnic peoples at a glance! Here, you only need a morning or afternoon to get to know them all! This exhibition is fun

whether you listen to traditional music, watch the water puppets with their damp and cheerful show or scale a longhouse of the Ede ethnic tribe in the giant open-air section. The original life-size models of the minority tribes are outside, but traditional costumes, musical instruments and handicraft also display the great variety of ethnic peoples. Because of the many figures and puppets, this museum will also fascinate kids until the end of the ethnic round tour. *Tue–Sun 8.30am–5.30pm | admission approx. 40,000 dong | Nguyen Van Huyen, on the northern outskirts on the route to the airport (journey time 25 minutes) | www.vme.org.vn*

HO CHI MINH HOUSE (142 A2) *(𝄞 0)*

Long queues regularly form outside the wooden house, where Ho Chi Minh lived from 1958 until his death in 1969. So any insights into the life of "Bac Ho" (or Uncle Ho) from the rather sparse office, the no less spartan bedroom and the pond, where he often sat and mused, can be time limited. *Daily 8am–11am, 1.30pm–4pm | admission approx. 40,000 dong | Ba Dinh Square | next to the Presidential Palace (in the park)*

HO CHI MINH MAUSOLEUM ● (142 A2) *(𝄞 0)*

Built between 1973 and 1975, the massive blocks of red, black and grey marble create an awe-inspiring memorial for the last resting place of Ho Chi Minh's embalmed body. In silence and usually in a long queue, visitors parade past the glass coffin containing the mortal remains of the country's great revolutionary hero. It was here on the ● *Ba Dinh Square* in front of the mausoleum, where on 2 September 1945, Ho Chi Minh declared Vietnam's independence. With full military pomp, a flag is hoisted every morning at 6am and then lowered

again at 9pm. *April–beginning of Sept Tue–Thu 7.30am–10.30am, Sat, Sun 7.30am–11am, beginning of Dec–Mar Tue–Thu 8–11, Sat, Sun 8am–11.30am (beginning of Sept–beginning of Dec mostly closed) | admission free | no admission in shorts, miniskirts and tank tops | cameras to be handed in*

HO HOAN KIEM ★ (143 D3–4) *(𝄞 0)*

Imagine you are strolling around the lake, it's still early and the water is covered in mist. Suddenly, a gleaming golden turtle appears; it carries a glinting sword. Unlikely? If you look for long enough at the water, you could believe it, like the Vietnamese. Legend has it that in the 15th century at the "Lake of the Returned Sword" the heroic Le Loi took a magical sword from a golden turtle in the lake and used it to drive the Chinese out of Vietnam. Having successfully done that, the magic sword was seized from Le Loi's sheath and restored to the turtle in the lake. As a gesture of gratitude, the *Thap Rua*, or Turtle Tower, was built on an island in the middle of the lake. Incidentally, for decades a 200 kg/440 lbs giant softshell turtle really lived in the lake – it died at a grand age in 2016.

● Every morning between 5am and 7am, the lakeside resembles a fitness centre, as joggers, gymnasts, plus tai chi and aerobic enthusiasts meet to get their daily fix of exercise. It costs nothing to join in. In the evenings, it's more hip-hop and breakdance.

INSIDER TIP ► "TUBE HOUSE" IN MA MAY STREET (143 D3) *(𝄞 0)*

Slip on felt slippers, shuffle ahead and be amazed: This wooden house dating from the 19th century is in fine shape. The *Ngoi Nha Di San Heritage House* was restored and opened to visitors as a typical example of this kind of very narrow building, known as a "tube house", that can be 60–80 m/197–262.5 ft long. The finely carved swing doors, the brick carvings, which promise a long life, and on the upper floor the beautiful antique bed with mother-of-pearl decorations are well preserved. *Daily 8am–5pm | admission approx. 13,000 dong | 87 Ma May*

VAN MIEU ★ ● (142 B4) (*ɒ 0*)

You might not get this close to Confucius ever again: step through only four gates to see the wise man. Ly Thanh Tong, the third ruler of the Ly Dynasty, had this Temple of Literature built in 1070 in honour of Confucius. Only six years later Vietnam's first university was founded in an adjoining property: Quoc Tu Giam, the Institute for "Sons of the State". The path begins at Quoc Tu Giam street, thereafter it passes through the *Van Mieu Portal* in the forecourt. The paved path leads up to the *Dai Trung* gate, the "Gate of the Great Middle", and then to the *Khue Van Cac*, the "Pleiades Gate", a pavilion dating from 1805. Literary debates and poetry readings were held here. In the court-

yard at the rear, stone turtles, symbols of wisdom, are clustered around the *Thien Quang Tinh*, the "Well of Heavenly Clarity". They bear 82 stone stelae, dating from between 1442 and 1779, inscribed with the names of the Confucian Academy's successful graduates.

Pass through the *Dai Thanh Gate* ("Gate of Great Success") and enter the fourth, most important courtyard in the temple buildings and the ceremonial hall honouring Confucius' 72 wisest disciples. Behind it is the fifth and final court, *Thai Hoc*, where you will find a museum and on the second floor altars with statues of the kings Ly Nhan Tong, Ly Thanh Tong and Le Thanh Tong. *Daily 7.30am–5.30pm | admission approx. 26,000 dong*

CITADEL (142 B–C 2–3) (*ɒ 0*)

For over 50 years it was a closed off as a military zone, but the first rebuilt sections are now open to the public. Completed between 1802 and 1812, it was built on the orders of Emperor Gia Long to a design drawn up by French military architects. So it was not difficult for the French

A centre for Confucian scholarship: the Van Mieu Temple of Literature

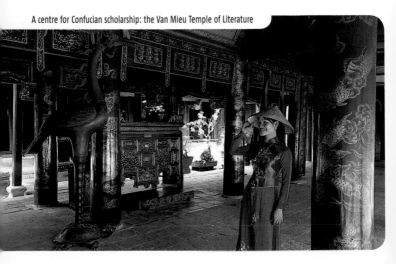

in 1872 to capture the stronghold and destroy most of it. Visitors can enter the inner citadel via the *Doan Mon* central gate *(19c Hoang Dieu)* on the western side at the level of the *Ho Chi Minh Mausoleum*. *Tue–Sun 8am–5pm | admission approx. 26,000 dong | www.hoangthanhthan glong.vn/en*

FOOD & DRINK

There are a number of good food stalls on the western edge of the Old Quarter in *Tong Duy Tan* and *Cam Chi*, about 500 m/ 1,640 ft north-east of the station. Outside the Old Quarter, there are food and *pho* soup stalls, in *Le Van Huu* (143 D–E5) *(Ø 0)*, for example. Many restaurants in Hanoi are closed between 2pm and 6pm.

BUN CHA DAC KIM (142 C3) *(Ø 0)*

One of Hanoi's top food stands – try the *bun cha* (pork meatballs with rice noodles) and the delicious *nem* (spring rolls). *1 Hang Manh | Budget*

CAFÉ BAR NOLA (143 D3) *(Ø 0)*

This three-floor artsy café with a rooftop terraces is hidden away in a courtyard. Sit back and relax with a good cup of coffee, wine or cocktails. A few snacks and some simple dishes plus WiFi are also available. *89 Ma May | tel. 024 39 26 46 69 | mobile 093 4 68 84 11 | Budget*

INSIDER TIP ► CONG CAPHE (142 B4) *(Ø 0)*

The café with vintage design impresses with the slightly murky charm of an opium den – between stylish "bullet holes", lounge cushions, black-and-white photos and colourful propaganda posters. Of course, fine quality stimulants: you should definitely try the coconut iced coffee! *4 Ly Thuong Kiet | opposite the Mercure Hotel | tel. 024 37 33 99 66 | Budget*

FOODSHOP 45 (142 B1) *(Ø 0)*

Well away from all the traffic, the idyllic INSIDER TIP ► Lake Truc Bach is the perfect place to take a quiet stroll – you can even hear the birds singing… and then sample the best Indian food in north Vietnam courtesy of the two brothers, Cuong and Hue. Relaxed atmosphere with sunset views. *59 Truc Bach | near the West Lake | tel. 024 37 16 29 59 | foodshop45. com | Budget*

HIGHWAY 4 (143 D3) *(Ø 0)*

Café bar with the best self-distilled brandies in the whole of Vietnam. Marvellous north Vietnamese cuisine, including specialities from the hill tribes. Cookery courses. Several branches. *5 Hang Tre | tel. 024 39 26 42 00 | www.highway4.com | Moderate*

INDOCHINE (143 D6) *(Ø 0)*

Award-winning Vietnamese cuisine at its finest in elegant surroundings with traditional musical accompaniment. Popular with coach parties at lunch-time. *38 Thi Sach | tel. 024 39 42 40 97 | www.indo chinehanoi.com | Expensive*

LA VERTICALE (143 D5) *(Ø 0)*

Five-star chef Didier Corlou conjures up some highly desirable creations. *19 Ngo Van So | tel. 024 39 44 63 17 | www.didier corlou-hanoirestaurants.com | Expensive*

LE BON STEAK HOUSE (143 E4) *(Ø 0)*

The pleasant garden restaurant with spacious interior offers international dishes, juicy steaks, a salad and breakfast buffet. Unfortunately, wine is only ordered by the bottle. Live music from 9pm. *1 Pham Ngu Lao | tel. 024 39 33 88 66 | www.le bonsteak.com.vn | Moderate*

SAWADEE (142 C6) *(Ø 0)*

A fantastic Thai restaurant serving delicacies from Vietnam's neighbour. Dining on two floors – on the upper level on a small veranda. *141 Ba Trieu | mobile tel. 090 2222141 | sawasdee.vn | Budget– Moderate*

SHOPPING

Hang Gai, Hang Bong and Hang Trong are *streets in the Old Quarter* with many tailors and shops selling silk products. Hang Gai and Hang Bom also specialise in galleries and crafts, around St Jo-

children. *43–51 Van Mieu | near the Temple of Literature | www.craftlink.com.vn*

DONG XUAN MARKET ●
(142 C2) (*∅ 0*)
The huge market with market hall sells hats, shirts, fruit, vegetables, karaoke systems and much more – until midnight.

HANOI GALLERY (143 D3) (*∅ 0*)
Colourful galleries lie around every corner in the old part of town, this one spe-

Red is the colour of happiness – colourful souvenirs in Hanoi's Old Quarter

seph's Cathedral. In Na Tho and Hang Trong you'll find some rather expensive boutiques, while Luong Van Can is the place for bespoke *ao dais*. That's not forgetting Hang Bac (silverware, jewellery, propaganda posters and crafts from the hill tribes), Lan Ong (herbal remedies) and Hang Buom (sweets).

CRAFT LINK AND HOA SEN GALLERY ☑
(142 B4) (*∅ 0*)
You can buy crafts (especially woven fabrics from the tribal hills) and some beautiful souvenirs. The proceeds go to projects supporting minorities and Hanoi street

cializes in propaganda posters. Some other vendors of these trendy souvenirs can be found at the Hang Bac. *62 Hang Buom*

MEKONG QUILTS ☑ (143 D3) (*∅ 0*)
Wonderful wall- and bed covers, pillows, hammocks, baskets made from water hyacinth, and bamboo wheels – hand-made by women with disabilities. *13 Hang Bac | Old town | www.mekong-plus.com*

SPORTS & ACTIVITIES

Book organised excursions and tours to Hanoi's surroundings at:

Ocean Tours | (143 D3) *(₥ 0)* (22 Hang Bac and 82 Ma May | tel. 024 39 26 04 63 | www.oceantours.com.vn)*: A reliable operator for tours especially for young people, with parties, campfires and kayaking adventures.

Todeco (142 C2–3) *(₥ 0)* (91 a/5 Ly Nam De | tel. 024 62 68 01 95 | mobile 090 3 22 70 82 | www.todeco-vn.com*: Customised tours, English-speaking tour guides. The volunteers' association ● *Hanoi E-Buddies (hanoiebuddies.com.vn)* offers free tours in Hanoi. The students show sides of the city seldom seen by tourists in English-speaking tours and in passing exercise the language.

ENTERTAINMENT

It's all the rage to mix under the locals in the *bia hoi* bars – Vietnamese beer costs less than 50 cents here, so sit in the plastic chairs and take in the busy atmosphere of the Old Quarter.

BAR & JAZZ CLUB MINH'S
(143 E4) *(₥ 0)*

Bar owner Minh teaches saxophone at the Hanoi Conservatory, so you can expect some high-class live jazz here (daily from 9pm). *1 Trang Tien | www.minhjazz vietnam.com*

HANOI ROCK CITY (0) *(₥ 0)*
Concert venue, bar and beer garden: western bands play their music here, too, with jazz every Tuesday and everything from punk to hip-hop at the weekend. Things get going around 10pm (no cover until then). *27/52 To Ngoc Van | Tay Ho district | www.hanoirockcity.com*

INSIDER TIP MOJITO BAR & LOUNGE
(142 C3) *(₥ 0)*

The barkeepers at this cool and unique bar are called *mixologists* and whip up

the house special, the pho-cocktail, and other delights. *19 Nguyen Quang Bich*

OPERA HOUSE
(143 E4) *(₥ 0)*

The programme includes classical concerts, theatre performances (often in Vietnamese) and dance. For up-to-date listings, see, for example, Vietnam News. *Tickets from 208,000 dong | 1 Trang Tien | tel. 024 39 33 01 13 | hanoioperahouse. org.vn*

WATER PUPPET THEATRE
(143 D3) *(₥ 0)*

Eleven actors operate the puppets to music played by wooden flutes, gongs, drums and the *dan bau*, the single-string box zither. You can see a fisherman struggling with his prey, you hear the rice growing, watch a jaguar hunt ducks and encounter fire-breathing dragons. Performances usually last for over an hour. *Thang Long Water Puppet Theatre | five shows daily 3pm–8pm, in winter four shows from 4pm | admission 52,000–104,000 dong (buy your ticket well in advance) | 57b Dinh Tien Doang | tel. 024 39 36 43 35 | www.thanglong waterpuppet.org and at the smaller Lotus Water Puppet Theatre) (0) (₥ 0) (admission approx. 104,000 dong | 16 Le Thai Tho | mobile 097 2 030 420)*

WHERE TO STAY

INSIDER TIP GREEN MANGO (0) *(₥ 0)*
Boutique hotel near the West Lake in a lively nightlife quarter with plenty of bars. The Nguyens give their guests a warm welcome: five floors (no lift) of stylishly furnished rooms and apartments, some with parquet flooring, balconies and large, glass (!) bathrooms. The ☼ suite with a sea view is impressive. The restaurant *(Expensive)* creates

Asian nouvelle cuisine. *20 rooms | 18/52 To Ngoc Van | Tay-Ho District | tel. 024 39 28 99 15 | Facebook: GreenMango Hanoi | Moderate*

INSIDER TIP ▶ LA BELLE VIE
(142 C1) (∅ 0)
Luxury at a low price: if you cannot decide between the old town or West Lake, you're in the right place – in the middle! Close to idyllic Lake Truc Bach and the night market, the hotel is highly rated for elegant rooms and an excellent breakfast. Don't miss the roof-top pool. *40 rooms | 105 Nguyen Truong To | Ba Dinh District | tel. 024 39 27 55 15 | mobile tel. 097 2 96 46 76 | www.labellevie hotel.com | Moderate–Expensive*

INSIDER TIP ▶ HANOI BOUTIQUE
HOTEL 1 (142–143 C–D2) (∅ 0)
A central location – but you can sleep in without being disturbed: modern, parquet-floor rooms and suites with flat screen TV, some rather small in plush 1950s style. ✂ Room 704 on the 7th floor is a lovely, quiet deluxe room with view. French/Vietnamese restaurant. *56 rooms | 7 Ngo Gach | tel. 024 39 33 22 88 | www.hanoiboutiquehotel.vn | Budget–Moderate*

HANOI LEGACY (143 D3) (∅ 0)
A mini hotel with a Roman neoclassic touch in the Old Quarter with reasonable rooms and even a lift. *25 rooms | 108 Hang Bac | tel. 024 39 35 26 62 | www.hanoilegacyhotel.com | Moderate*

LUCKY 2 HOTEL
(142 C3) (∅ 0)
Rooms furnished in Vietnamese style with satellite TV and telephone. There's another Lucky Hotel in *Hang Trong no. 12. 22 rooms | 46 Hang Hom | tel. 024 3 92 81 70 | luckyhotel.com.vn | Moderate*

SOFITEL LEGEND METROPOLE
(143 D4) (∅ 0)
The best hotel in town. Stay in the renovated old wing and bask in the opulence of the colonial era. The *Opera Wing*, opened in 1996, may be more luxurious, but less atmospheric. The ● chocolate buffet in the afternoon is stupendous. *364 rooms | 15 Ngo Quyen | tel. 024 38 26 69 19 | www.accorhotels.com | Expensive*

TAM HOTEL (142 B1) (∅ 0)
This small hotel is situated in a wonderfully peaceful residential area on Lake Truc Bach. Pretty, spacious rooms with laminate flooring and balconies, a rooftop bar and a professional travel agency in-house. *25 rooms | 3–5 Tran Te Xuong | tel. 024 37 15 40 69 | www.tamhotel.com. vn | Budget–Moderate*

INFORMATION

Vietnam Tourism (Vietnam National Administration of Tourism) **(142 C5) (∅ 0)** *(80 Quan Su | Hoan Kiem district | tel. 024 39 42 37 60 | www.vietnamtourism.com)*

WHERE TO GO

CHUA THAY AND CHUA TAY PHUONG
★ **(137 D3) (∅ E3)**
Situated in the heart of a fertile, rice-growing area, approx. 40 km/24.9 mi west of Hanoi, only a few kilometres apart, are these two magnificent pagodas *(admission to each approx. 26,000 dong)*.

The ✂ *Chua Tay Phuong* near the village of Thach Xa stands on a hillock but to reach it, you will have to climb around 260 steps. The three ironwood buildings have elegant upward-sweeping eaves, beautifully adorned with all kinds of dragons and other mythical creatures – phoenix, ky lan and turtles. Visitors also get to admire 62 precious statues, among them the 18 *la han* ("enlightened ones"), masterfully carved from the wood of the jack fruit tree. Situated by Lake Long Tri near the village of Sai Son at the foot of a limestone peak and surrounded by temples and pavilions is *Chua Thay* or the "Master's Pagoda". It is dedicated to the miracle-worker and sorcerer, Tu Dao, who withdrew to the mountain in the 12th century to meditate and to disseminate the teachings of the Buddha. Tu Dao is also the patron saint of water puppeteers.

CUC PHUONG NATIONAL PARK
(137 D4) (Ø E3)
Vietnam's largest jungle park! Situated some 120 km/75 mi south-west of Hanoi, you can find some giant 1,000-year-old trees, squirrels, countless butterflies and hundreds of different bird species. The rocky outcrops rise to a height of 600 m/1,969 ft. No fewer than ten trekking trails criss-cross this unique primeval forest. The Delacour's langur, originally thought to be extinct, was rediscovered here and is now bred in a small *monkey sanctuary (Endangered Primate Rescue Center | daily 9am–11am and 1.30pm–4pm | www.primatecenter.org)*. Facilities, including hotels, villas, a camp-site and restaurants (usually full at the weekend), are situated in the park. Oct–Dec and March/April are the best months for a visit. A few kilometres from the park entrance, the *Cuc Phuong Resort & Spa (70 rooms | Dong Tam | mobile 0125 2 72 79 79 | cucphuongresort.vn | Expensive)* offers rustic twin bungalows and a pool. *Admission (with guide for the Primate Center) approx. 91,000 dong | tel. 0229 3 84 80 06 | www.cucphuongtourism.com*

HOA BINH AND HUONG TICH SON
(137 D3–4) (Ø E3)
Hoa Binh is a rather nondescript provincial capital, approx. 75 km/46.6 mi south-west of Hanoi. Most of the visitors are locals, who come to these parts to ex-

Alive and kicking: a Delacour's langur at the Cuc Phuong National Park

plore the Muong hill tribe's villages, such as *Ban Dam* or *Giang Mo,* and to admire the impressive, stilted longhouses. The *Mai Chau valley* is home to a number of minorities, including the Black and mainly White Thai. If you would like a conducted tour, you are advised to hire a guide (charge approx. 260,000 dong).

Then, it becomes almost mystical and wonderful: hidden away in ★ *Huong Tich Son* (Mountain of Fragrant Vestiges) is the Huong Tich Cave with the *Perfume Pagoda (Chua Huong),* which was built in honour of the Goddess of Mercy, Quan Am. You have to experience Vietnam's

Number One place of pilgrimage – if possible, not for the New Year festival! Up to 60,000 visitors daily are rowed in 5,000 boats to the magnificent limestone landscape. That puts an end to a romantic atmosphere, or rather: romance gets lost in a fun water fight, including the traffic jam on the river and the busy festival. You have to take a boat trip (many people make this tour as a day trip from Hanoi, from approx. 338,000 dong). A cable car takes visitors up to the pagoda complex grotto on the mountain. Alternatively, you can make the strenuous, approx. two-hour climb (sturdy shoes essential).

some 90 km/55.9 mi south of Hanoi has become a top tourist attraction. The limestone formations, which have emerged over millennia, are compara-

The mountains around Sa Pa are perfect for hiking

ble in beauty with Ha Long Bay – the difference being, there's no sea. In the heart of this spectacular landscape lies the provincial capital of *Ninh Binh*. Despite a population of around 60,000, the town was formerly not much more than a pretty village. But that changed when independent travellers discovered the region. The most popular spot is the town of *Tam Coc (admission approx. 91,000 dong | 10 km/6.2 mi west of Ninh Binh)*, where the boats *(for four people approx. 104,000 dong per person)* for the tours along the river are moored. At the *Nguyen Shack (5 rooms | Tam Coc | at Khe Ha village | tel. 0229 3 61 86 78 | www. nguyenshack.com | Budget)*, you stay in a breathtaking valley on the lake in palm-frond huts. For more comfort: *Emeralda*

HA LONG BAY ON LAND ★
(137 D4) (ℳ E4)
The perfect fairy tale scenery: rising abruptly and seemingly without any base from a sea of dark green are wooded cones, rocky tips and mountain ridges. So it's no surprise that karst landscape,

Ninh Binh *(172 rooms, some with private pool | Van Long Reserve | Gia Van | mobile 096 8 69 96 90 | www.emeraldresort. com | Expensive)*, lying amidst the rice paddies like a temple. *Information in the hotels and on arrival in Tam Coc*

SA PA

(136 B2) (∅ C2) **Above the clouds: around hair-raising bends and endless zigzags through the majestic mountain landscape surrounding ⭐ Sa Pa – the colourful world of the hill tribes awaits you.** Sa Pa (pop. 40,000) was developed by the French about 100 years ago as a spa and military sanatorium. Pretty villas, fortress-like country houses and a church recall the colonial era. Although the town is a remote spot and the coldest and mistiest place in Vietnam (best time to visit: Sept–Nov), it has become a bustling tourist destination.

The little town is spread across hilly terrain at a height of 1,560 m/5,118 ft at the foot of the Fan Si Pan (Phan Si Pang), a mountain often shrouded by low cloud, the Alpine Hoang Lien Son range forming the backdrop. Among the long-standing traditions of the hill tribes are the construction of stilt houses, a belief in natural spirits, betel nut chewing, tooth blackening and eyebrow shaving. Many of the people here no longer wear the colourfully embroidered traditional dress with heavy silver jewellery – mostly just women don this clothing, often only on market days or holidays.

The usual way to reach the town is in a bus from Hanoi (in 5–6 hours) or via Lao Cai (37 km/23 mi north-east of Sa Pa), reachable on the railway line from 1922, e.g. on the elegant INSIDER TIP Victoria Express *(only for guests of the Victoria Sa Pa | journey time 8–9 hrs | return ticket* from 3,120,000 dong | free hotline tel. 18 00 59 99 55 | www.victoriahotels.asia). There are also regular daily services to Lao Cai. Then take a scheduled bus or tourist coach on to Sa Pa.

SIGHTSEEING

HILL VILLAGE AND WATERFALLS

Easy walks via suspension bridges and through terraced paddy fields lead into the surrounding countryside, e.g. to the impressive *Cat Cat waterfall (admission approx. 65,000 dong | approx. 3 km/1.9 mi to the west)* in a bamboo forest and to the *Thac Bac* or Silver Waterfall *(approx. 10 km/6.2 mi to the west)*, which drops from about 100 m/328 ft in three stages. The walks pass through the villages of the hill tribes, where there is accommodation – e.g. in *Ta Phin* (Village of the Red Dao) – or else you can take a stroll through the delightful Ta Van valley into the village of *Ta Van*. In the village of *Cat Cat*, near to the waterfall, you can watch the Hmong women at work on their weaving and embroidery. Blue dresses and turban-style headwear are the characteristic features of Hmong clothing, which they still make themselves and then dye with indigo.

MARKETS

The *Sapa market (daily 7am–6pm | Dien Bien Phu | above the Lake Sa Pa)* has moved into a two-storey hall (1st floor: lots of textiles and silver jewellery). There are equally lively markets in the vicinity on other days, where people pf the hill tribes meet each other. Mainly women belonging to the Black Hmong tribe wander the streets and alleys of Sa Pa to sell their hand-embroidered goods to tourists. Not only do they have a good command of French and English, they also deploy some sophisticated sales techniques.

FOOD & DRINK

THE HILL STATION SIGNATURE RESTAURANT ☆
How about some dried water buffalo meat with chillies or pan-fried bamboo as a snack? You can sit on the floor or on a chair and enjoy the ethnic cuisine of northern Vietnam with a view of the mountains. *37 Phan Si Phan | tel. 0214 3 88 71 11 | www.thehillstation.com | Expensive*

NATURE BAR & GRILL ●
Eat well in Vietnamese style (from the grill, vegetarian, even a little hint of Italian) by a warming hearth over a beer, a cocktail or a punch – the perfect spot on a cold winter's evening. *24 Cau May (2nd floor) | tel. 091 2 27 00 68 | Moderate*

SPORTS & ACTIVITIES

The *Fan Si Pan (Phan Si Pang)*, at 3,143 m/ 10,312 ft Vietnam's highest mountain, is situated in the north of *Hoang Lien Son Nature Reserve*, known mainly for its varied range of bird species.

Sa Pa has rapidly changed – it has embraced luxury! Instead of outside toilets, there are heated toilet seats and roof-top pools, instead of tea, Nescafé is served at the homestay, and instead of exhausting treks lasting two- to three-days, the cable cars go non-stop to Fan Si Pan: a *cable car (daily 7.30am–5.30pm, about 572,000 dong per person | fansipanlegend.sunworld.vn)* takes 20 minutes to reach the mountain station; from here, the summit is a climb up another 600 steps.

WHERE TO STAY

BAMBOO SAPA ☆
Comfortable rooms (some with balcony and mock-fireplace, mountain panorama included) in this five-storey hotel. Also a good travel agency on the premises. *56 rooms | 18 Muang Hoa | tel. 0214 3 87 10 75 | www.bamboosapahotel.com. vn | Moderate*

THAI BINH SAPA
Nice, family-run hotel on the outskirts, but quiet and warm (electric blankets, fireplace). Tours and guides. *14 rooms |*

FOR BOOKWORMS AND FILM BUFFS

Sunday Menu – (2005) Ironic short stories told from the point of view of a young Vietnamese woman, Pham Thi Hoai, about everyday life in Hanoi

The Lover – Novel (1984) by Marguerite Duras, who was born in what was then Indochina. The film was made in 1991 by Jean-Jacques Annaud as the erotic story of a 15-year-old French girl and an older, wealthy Vietnamese man

Films about the **Vietnam war** include Oscar-winning "Apocalypse Now", comedy-drama "Good Morning, Vietnam", as well as "The Deer Hunter", "Platoon" and "Coming Home"

The Scent of Green Papaya – About a young girl in the 1950s who begins to work as a servant for a wealthy family. This drama became the first internationally successful Vietnamese film and even got nominated for an Academy Award

Green, blue, red, violet – traditional clothing in Bac Ha market

5 Ham Rong | tel. 020 3 87 12 12 | www. thaibinhhotel.com | Budget

TOPAS ECOLODGE ☼ ◉
Lots of natural materials, solar energy and waste-water treatment, even for the eco-friendly heated infinity pool: the French-Vietnamese hotel offers rustic-style, but very comfortable chalets. Plus a stunning panorama from above the clouds. *25 rooms | 24 Muong Hoa | Thanh Kim (approx. 15 km/9.3 mi south-east of Sa Pa, 45 mins on a gravel track) | tel. 0214 3 87 13 31 | www.topasecolodge. com | Expensive*

VICTORIA SAPA ☼
You'll find the best first class hotel, in rustic chalet style, on the outskirts. The rooms are comfortable, some with four-poster bed and balcony. Other amenities include tennis court, badminton and a heated indoor pool. *76 rooms | free hot-*

line tel. 18 00 59 99 55 | www.victoria hotels.asia | Expensive

Sa Pa Tourism (2 Phan Xi Pan | on the way out of town towards the Cat Cat water-fall | tel. 0214 3 87 19 75 | www.sapa-tour ism.com)

WHERE TO GO

BAC HA (136 C1) (*⌘ D2*)
This small town (pop. 3,000) lies about 100 km/62 mi north-east of Sa Pa at an altitude of 900 m/2,953 ft. It's a part of the country famed for its lively *market* – a sea of green, blue, red and vio-let –, which draws tourists in on Sunday. Everyone wants to see and photograph the "flower Hmong" *(Hmong Hoa)*, so called because of their multi-coloured clothing adorned with floral motifs.

HUE AND THE CENTRE

The central region of Vietnam around the resort of Da Nang has no fewer than three important historical sites.

In addition to the old Imperial city of Hue with its Imperial citadel by the Song Huong, the Perfume River, and impressive imperial tombs, there are the enchanting ruins of the Champa complex in My Son and the largely Chinese market town of Hoi An, from the 17th century onwards an internationally important trading port by the South China Seas.

Always visible in central Vietnam is the Truong Son mountain range that runs parallel to the south coast for 1,000 km/620 mi. At no other point are the mountains closer to the sea than where the Bach Ma mountains form the dividing line between the subtropical north and the tropical south. If the region around Hue should live up to its reputation as the wettest in Vietnam, then you will simply have to make for Da Nang further south, where it is usually sunny. The port city is famous for its beaches and also the excellent Cham Museum, which sheds light on the ancient civilisation that once flourished here. During the Vietnam War, the magnificent Marble Mountains above Da Nang became a hide-out for the Vietcong guerrillas who gave the Americans good reasons to be fearful.

On the border with south Vietnam the uplands broaden out to the west. Thanks to its location at an altitude of 1,500 m/4,921 ft and a benign climate,

The Imperial Palace at Hue, endless white beaches and Hoi An's Old Quarter – the multifaceted central part of Vietnam

Da Lat is often justifiably described as the "City of Eternal Spring". No surprise then that this highland resort has become very popular especially with honeymooners.

BUON MA THUOT

(141 E1) *(𝄞 G10)* **Off the beaten track: ox carts instead of moped chaos and souvenir hunters; waterfalls instead of a concrete jungle. And not forgetting: cloud nine for all coffee addicts!**

You can sense that Buon Ma Thuot (pop. 200,000) grew out of a French military station first established in 1910. Many villas have survived from the times when the French chose the cooler uplands, at a height of about 500 m/1,640 ft, as their summer retreat. Buon Ma Thuot is the provincial capital of Dak Lak and is renowned for its coffee, generally considered to be the best in Vietnam.

The best beans come from the highlands: the coffee harvest in Buon Ma Thuot

SIGHTSEEING

MUSEUM OF ETHNOLOGY

If you are interested in the Ede, Hmong and Muong hill tribes, this museum (also called Dak Lak museum) provides good information. The INSIDER TIP gong collection is unique – you could easily overlook this because of the colourful traditional costumes, boats and stuffed wild animals. The centuries-old musical instruments are said to have a magical connection to the gods. You can hear gong music at folklore shows with the *Gong Dance* of the Muong tribe and at all the region's festivals. *Wed–Sun 7am–11am, 2am–5pm | admission approx. 26,000 dong | 182 Nguyen Du/corner of Le Duan*

INSIDER TIP TRUNG NGUYEN COFFEE MUSEUM (COFFEE VILLAGE)

More than 10,000 items depicting the global history of coffee, wonderfully presented in a lovely wooden longhouse. Shiny polished coffeemakers from the 19th century, antique coffee mills, and of course many small cafés serving the best coffee and selling fresh beans in *Coffee Village*. *Daily 7am–5pm | admission approx. 26,000 dong | Le Thanh Tong | approx. 3 km/1.9 mi from the centre*

FOOD & DRINK

BON TRIEU

Try the delicious *bon bay mon* – wafer-thin beef in sweet'n sour sauces. *33 Hai Ba Trung | mobile: 091 3 43 67 72 | Moderate*

WHERE TO STAY

DAM SAN HOTEL

Modern rooms, garden pool, tennis court. Some nice cafés nearby. *60 rooms | 212 Nguyen Cong Tru | tel. 0262 3 85 12 34 | damsanhotel.com.vn | Budget*

INFORMATION

Dak Lak Tourist (3 Phan Chu Trinh | tel. 0262 3 85 22 46 | www.daklaktourist. com.vn)

WHERE TO GO

Until World War II, the province of Dak Lak was used by the emperor as his hunting grounds – that's no surprise, as there's no other region in Vietnam with such a plentiful supply of game. There is also plenty of water. Some 27 km/16.8 mi south-west of Buon Ma Thuot, the cascading *Drai Sap falls (141 E1) (🕮 G10)* in the heart of a rainforest are an impressive sight, especially after heavy rainfall. In *Buon Tua* (Bon Tur) and *Buon Jang Lanh* you can get to meet members of the Ede hill tribe in their traditional long houses and stilt buildings. Also known as the Rhade, here mothers are heads of family; the clans live in longhouses. The famous *Jarai graves* have impressive wooden figures. *Lake Lak*

(141 E2) (🕮 G11) (about 50 km/31.1 mi south of Buon Ma Thuot) with its plentiful fish is an ideal habitat for storks, cranes and ducks. Most tourists are attracted here for rowing parties and bird-watching as well as elephant rides across the flat area by the lake, the same as in most other tourist sites in this province. For instance, in the "elephant villages" like *Ban Don* (45 km/28 mi north-west of Buon Ma Thuot), where elephants have been captured and tamed for centuries and nowadays have to "perform" at traditional festivals as footballers and at races. MARCO POLO recommends not participating in elephant tours and similar offers (see p. 23). Those who prefer going on safari nearby can join the guided tours in the *Yok Don National Park* (about 40 km/24.9 mi west of Buon Ma Thuot) where tigers are even supposed to roam alongside several remaining wild elephants – however, the tigers are probably on the edge of Vietnam's largest national park, which is inaccessible.

MARCO POLO HIGHLIGHTS

★ Da Lat
The lovers' city oozes colonial charm, while the surrounding area is a haven for active holidaymakers → p. 58

★ Po Klong Garai towers
The Cham perfected the art of temple construction → p. 59

★ Cham Museum
Relics from an ancient and unique culture in Da Nang → p. 61

★ My Son
In the middle of the jungle: the ruins of the Cham's temple complex → p. 63

★ Marble Mountains
Mysterious caves and pagodas, incense sticks and souvenirs – plus a fantastic all-round view from the top of Mount Thuy Son → p. 63

★ Hoi An
Picturesque rows of streets, trading houses and pagodas in the Old Quarter, plus much Chinese-Japanese-style charm → p. 64

★ Hue citadel
By the Perfume River – see for yourself the opulence and grandeur enjoyed by Vietnam's former rulers on a stroll through the site → p. 70

DA LAT

(141 E2) (*⊞ G11)* ★ **Da Lat (pop. 200,000) is variously described as the favourite spot for home-sick colonial rulers, tourist hotspot and honeymoon capital for Vietnamese newly-weds.**

The summer palace of the last Vietnamese emperor: Dinh 3 in Da Lat

The latter is due mainly to the fact that young Vietnamese couples regard lakes, waterfalls and forests as the epitome of romance, like the famous "Lake of Sighs". When in spring the cherry trees are in full pink blossom, the setting is perfect – the only downside being that it rains frequently here. It was in 1897 that the doctor Alexandre Yersin founded a sanatorium in this city, which sits at an altitude of 1,475 m/4,839 ft. It was another 15 years before the first Europeans settled here.

For the upper echelons of colonial society the smart Palace Hotel is until today the perfect place to spend the hot summer months in Vietnam. Those who could afford it, including the last Vietnamese emperor, Bao Dai, built villas in the pine forests above Lake Xuan Huong.

SIGHTSEEING

CHUA THIEN VUONG

The three yellow timber pagodas, built in 1958 by the Chaozhou Chinese community, stand on a hill surrounded by pine forests. Of particular interest here are the three approx. 4 m/13.1 ft high Buddha statues, which were donated by a British Buddhist from Hong Kong. They are made from gilded sandalwood and each one weighs around 1,400 kg/3,100 lbs. *Approx. 5 km/3.1 mi south-east of the city centre, via Khe San street*

SUMMER PALACE (DINH 3) ●

A yellow-brown villa with about 26 rooms, built in 1933, recalls the days of Bao Dai, Vietnam's last emperor, who ruled from 1926 to 1945. On display are the Imperial living rooms and many private photos. *Daily 7am–11am, 1.30pm–4pm | admission approx. 26,000 dong | 2 Le Hong Phong*

FOOD & DRINK

LE RABELAIS ✺

Gourmet restaurant with French-style food, a lake view, liveried waiters and piano music (from 7pm). *High Tea 4–5pm. 12 Tran Phu | at the Hotel Dalat Palace | tel. 0263 3 82 54 44 | Expensive*

THUY TA RESTAURANT ⤸

The restaurant occupies a magnificent spot (thus the a bit exaggerated pices): on stilts by Lake Xuan Huong. The view from here on sunny afternoons is just perfect. *1 Yersin | tel. 0263 3 82 22 88 | Moderate–Expensive*

SPORTS & ACTIVITIES

BIKING, TREKKING, FUN SPORTS

The pretty countryside and the pleasant climate provide just the right conditions for outdoor adventure – cycle tours (approx. 52,000 dong per day), a climb to the top of ⤸ *Mount Lang Biang* (with detours to the Lat villages), trekking, rock climbing, abseiling, paragliding and canyoning are just some of the options. Always check equipment and mountain bikes carefully beforehand. One recommended tour operator is *Phat Tire Ventures (109 Nguyen Van Troi | tel. 0263 3 82 94 22 | www.ptv-vietnam.com).*

MOTORCYCLE TOURS

The new Ho Chi Minh Highway brings you to some of the prettiest stretches of road in the highlands as it approaches the border to Laos, crossing over steep passes and whizzing through amazing scenery. A safe bet for tours is the *Dalat Easy Riders (c/o Easy Rider Café | 70 Phan Dinh Phung | day trip approx. US$20–35, 3-day tour incl. accommodation and snacks from approx. US$65–75 per day | www.dalat-easyrider.com).*

WHERE TO STAY

ANA MANDARA VILLAS DALAT & SPA

Magnificently restored colonial villas with discretely elegant furnishings and décor, heated pool, wine cellar, exclusive restaurant. It could hardly be more luxurious. *57 rooms | Le Lai | tel. 0263 3 55 58 88 | www.anamandara-resort.com | Expensive*

DALAT PALACE HERITAGE ⤸

A combination of luxury and nostalgia recalling the grandeur of the 1920s. Plus a great view over Lake Xuan Huong. *43 rooms | 12 Tran Phu | tel. 0263 3 82 54 44 | www.royaldl.com | Expensive*

INSIDER TIP ▶ TTC HOTEL NGOC LAN ⤸

Bargain alert! Here, you can almost always find a fabulous, reasonably priced room. An old cinema has been transformed into a mid-range hotel with smart rooms, some of which are huge (parquet floors) and have magnificent balcony views over the lake. The smaller rooms at the rear are quieter. Massage and fitness suite, superb location near the market. *91 rooms | 42 Nguyen Chi Thanh | tel. 0263 3 83 88 38 | www.ttchotels.com | Budget–Moderate*

INFORMATION

Dalat Tourist (1 Le Dai Hanh | mobile 098 1 16 60 88 | www.dalattourist.com.vn)

WHERE TO GO

PO KLONG GARAI TOWERS ★
(141 F3) (*m H11*)

Do you feel like a rendezvous with Shiva? Then, it's time to head for the coast in the former kingdom of the Cham. Spiky cacti surround the four chunky Cham towers of Po Klong Garai, situated approx. 65 km/40.4 mi south-east of Da Lat on the N 20 to Phan Rang. The best time to visit is September/October, when to celebrate their new year the Cham perform traditional songs and dances at the site. What is so surprising is the good condition of the buildings – the temples were built in the 13/14th under King Simhavarman III. You enter the complex through a beautifully decorated gateway. Adorning the inside the temple tower is a *mukha lingam*, a stylised phallus symbolising Shiva, who is depicted dancing for his subjects. *Daily 7.30am–6pm | admission approx. 13,000 dong*

WATERFALLS (141 E2) (*Ø G11*)

Leaving from the old station in Da Lat, approx. 500 m/1,640 ft east of Lake Xuan Huong, a train runs several times a day (*7.45am–4pm every two hours; minimum 20 people*) to the Linh Phuoc Pagoda in the town of *Trai Mat*. From here leads a 7 km/4.4 mi signposted trail to the beautiful *Tiger Waterfall (Thac Hang Cop | admission approx. 13,000 dong)*, where you will be greeted by a huge statue of a tiger. Not just the waterfalls, but also the town lakes are suffering badly from the high demands of the vast Da Nhim reservoir further west. The cascades are most impressive at the end of the rainy period (Nov/Dec). Other good examples include the *Prenn Waterfall (by the N 20, approx. 10 km/6.2 mi from Da Lat), the Lien Khuong Waterfall (N 20, approx. 30 km/18.6 mi towards Saigon), the Pongour Waterfall (by the N20, 45 km/ 28 mi towards Saigon)* and the huge *Dambri Waterfall* near *Bao Loc*. All waterfalls charge admission fees of approx. 26,000 dong

DA NANG

(139 E3) (*Ø G7*) Nobody passes this hub so quickly – Da Nang is the gateway to Hue, My Son and Hoi An. In the town itself, the unique Cham Museum will even have museum buffs in raptures!

On the section of road from Hue you will notice a distinct change in the climate once you have negotiated *Cloud Pass (Deo Hai Van)*, which acts as a meteorological divide. You will soon reach Da Nang, the rapidly growing provincial capital of approx. 1.1 million inhabitants.

Impressive natural spectacle – Pongour Waterfall near Da Lat

WHERE TO START?
Savour the atmosphere on Da Nang's lively **Bach Dang Promenade** beside the River Han; then head north from the Cham Museum, past old villas, hotels, the market and the tourist information office. Everything is accessible on foot – if you're coming from a beach hotel, take a (moped) taxi over the Dragon Bridge, which is beautifully illuminated at night.

However, it's still an amazing puzzle: a god with an elephant head (Ganesha), female breasts as the "primeval mother" (Uroja), a phallus as god (Shiva). The religious art of the Cham created a mystical world, where Shiva dances, Vishnu meditates, lions and elephants unite to become remarkable mythical creatures and the goddess of fertility looks on at all the tohubohu.

Founded in 1915 by the French, this small, but rather fine museum houses the world's best and largets collection of

Because it occupies a favourable location at the mouth of the River Han, Da Nang has always been an important port. In 1965, the Americans occupied the town and set about developing what was to become one of their largest air bases in south-east Asia. China Beach is renowned for its high waves – during the war American soldiers came here to surf when they had "rest and relaxation" time.

SIGHTSEEING

CAO DAI TEMPLE ●
Like the Holy See in Tay Ninh, the Cao Dai Temple here, the second-largest in the country, is an impressive sight. Access is strictly segregated by sex. Women enter the shrine on the left, men on the right. Priests are allowed to use the central entrance. Behind the altar the "divine eye" made from a huge glass ball watches the faithful at prayer. *Services daily at 6am, noon, 6pm and midnight | admission free | near the station on Hai Phong*

CHAM MUSEUM ★ ●
Prepare to experience a showcase of the gods, as three world religions meet in the Cham kingdom – Hinduism, Buddhism and Islam. But it's quite peaceful.

Dance of gods: sandstone relief from Da Nang's Cham Museum

Cham artefacts, many of which are sandstone sculptures. You should set aside at least two hours to cover what is a clearly arranged set of displays. No less than eight hundred years of civilisation are

Breakfast Vietnamese-style – noodle soup is a speciality in Hoi An

BROTHER'S CAFÉ HOI AN
An idyllic spot by the Thu Bon River. Relax in a colonial villa with a tropical garden, airy wooden interior and exposed beams and enjoy good Vietnamese or international cuisine. Well-stocked wine cellar. Book your table in the evening. *27 Phan Boi Chau | tel. 0235 3 91 41 50 | brother cafehoian.com.vn | Expensive*

LITTLE FAIFO
In this wonderful old town restaurant, after a champagne welcome, you dine on two levels to the sound of piano music (booking essential for the balcony) and enjoy fine quality local cuisine. The prawns in ginger-tamarind sauce are tasty as well as the cheesecake. *66 Nguyen Thai Hoc | tel. 0235 3 91 74 44 | www.littlefaifo.com | Moderate*

SON HOI AN
The whole Son family is busy in this kitchen. A rustic and romantic Slow Food restaurant among palm trees and rice paddies serving lovingly plated dishes (mostly Vietnamese food and barbecue) with soft jazz music. *232 Cua Dai | tel. 0235 3 86 11 72 | mobile 090 5 70 71 44 | Moderate*

Hoi An is famed for its bespoke tailoring service (order in time, preferably with a template) and for silk, most of which comes from China. One metre of natural silk, 90 cm wide, costs approx. 235,000 dong.

HOI AN HANDICRAFT WORKSHOP
For souvenirs, crafts and performances of traditional music (10.15am and 3.15pm). *9 Nguyen Thai Hoc*

MR. XE
The place to go for a perfect fit, right on time, and with proper prices. Another well-known and professional, but also more expensive shop with excellent goods and quality in the same street is

Yaly (No. 47 | www.yalycouture.com). 71 Nguyen Thai Hoc | tel. 0235 3 91 03 88

REACHING OUT 🕲

Disabled artisans make and sell some beautiful items in this historic building (e.g. handbags, jewellery, clothing, toys). *103 Nguyen Thai Hoc | next to the Tan Ky house | www.reachingoutvietnam.com*

SILK ROAD

Good Old Quarter boutique where tailor Thuy magics up blouses, clothes and trousers from 520,000 dong, depending on material and size. *91 Nguyen Thai Hoc | tel. 0235 3 91 10 58*

LEISURE, SPORTS & BEACH

BOAT TOURS

Take a paddle boat tour along the Thu Bon River, the largest of the province, and explore the artisan and fishing villages in the vicinity *(one-hour tours cost from approx. 52,000 dong).*

COOKERY COURSES ●

Many restaurants offer cookery courses, some with a visit to the market included, e.g. *Vy's Cooking School in the Morning Glory (106 Nguyen Thai Hoc | tel. 0235 3 91 12 27 | tastevietnam.asia)*, *Brothers Café, Tam Tam,* or, including an atmospheric boat tour on the Thu Bon River, INSIDER TIP ▶ *Red Bridge Restaurant (Thon 4 | Cam Thanh | approx. 4 km/2.5 mi from the centre | tel. 0510 3 93 32 22 | www.visithoian.com).*

INSIDER TIP ▶ PAPER LANTERN COURSES 🕲

If you have a knack for crafts, you can lean how to make your own paper lanterns in Hoi An. The lanterns make for a lovely souvenir or Christmas present, and you'll also be supporting a project to help disabled individuals find work. *Lifestart Foundation (14 Nguyen Thai Hoc | www.lifestartfoundation.org.au)* offers courses for approx. 702,000 dong.

At the end of the day, it's time to light the lanterns in Hoi An

INFORMATION

Vietnam Tourism (14 Nguyen Van Cu | tel. 0234 3 81 83 16)

WHERE TO GO

INSIDER TIP BACH MA NATIONAL PARK
☼ (139 D–E3) (*∅ G7*)
Waterfalls, emerald-coloured natural pools and fantastic views! Here, you can get active and try trekking, climbing and abseiling. You can also take it at a more leisurely pace and hike through the national park situated 40 km/24.9 mi south-east of Hue. But most tours to the impressive waterfalls, lakes and the 1,444 m/4,738 ft mountain peak are not for those who appreciate home comforts – the leeches in the rainforest (signposted, approx. 3–4 hours, hiking shoes essential!) happily welcome every visitor. It is usually full and very noisy at weekends. For information on accommodation in six basic guesthouses (*Budget*): tel. 0234 3 87 13 30. Park March–Sept 7am–5pm, Oct–Feb. 7.30am–4.30pm | admission approx. 520,000 dong, 5-hour trip from Hue from approx. 780,000 dong | www.bachmapark.com.vn

CHUA THIEN MU (139 D3) (*∅ G7*)
A legend has grown up around the "Heavenly Lady Pagoda" (5 km/3.1 mi west of the city on the northern bank of the Perfume River). It is said that in 1601 the figure of an elderly lady appeared on a hill before the founder of the Nguyen dynasty, Nguyen Hoang. She insisted that this place belonged to a deity and demanded that a pagoda be built here. Nguyen Hoang obeyed and the country and the Nguyen family prospered for hundreds of years. In 1844 Emperor Thieu Tri added the octagonal, 21 m/68.9 ft high *Phuoc Duyen tower*. Buddha statues are distributed across seven levels, with each level dedicated to a *manushi*-buddha (a Buddha in human form). The tower has become a symbol for Hue.
A monk by the name of Thich Quang Duc, who practised in Thien Mu, caused a stir in 1963. He drove a light blue Austin car, now occupying a building to the rear of the pagoda, to Saigon and in protest at the cruelty of the Diem regime set himself on fire before the world's press.

IMPERIAL TOMBS (LANG KHAI DINH) (139 D3) (*∅ G7*)
Don't expect the Taj Mahal! But you can already sense the pomp and flair of

LOW BUDGET

Unbeatable bargains in Hue are the ten rooms (from 312,000 dong) at the *Sunny C Hotel (7/25 Hai Ba Trung | mobile 091 6 00 30 92 and 094 2 95 20 77)* with TV, some with balconies, breakfast in bed or on the terrace.

Banh trang trung? Pizza! Thin and crispy and, of course: made of rice dough. The crêpe-like *banh ep* (with cucumbers, papaya, herbs) are a street-food trend. Where? In Hue, e. g. in the historic Phu Cat district: *20 and 44 Nguyen Du (side street off Chi Lang Street)* and *14 Le Thanh Ton*. Costs: both less than 13,000 dong.

You can hardly miss the *Bun Bo Hue restaurants (e.g. 11b Ly Thuong Kiet | tel. 0234 3 82 64 60)*. The name says it all – you eat what arrives on the table. A bowl of *bun bo hue* is a typically Hue-style beef and rice noodle soup (approx. 26,000 dong).

long forgotten times, a pinch of feng-shui harmony and a feeling of morbid romanticism.

All the tombs were built to a similar pattern. Most of them are enclosed by a wall and are lined by an honour courtyard with stone elephants, horses and civil and military mandarins. Each one has a stele pavilion in which the achievements of the deceased emperor are engraved on a marble tablet. Behind the pavilion is a temple for worshipping the Imperial family and then there's the mausoleum with the emperor's remains.

The Tomb of *Tu Duc* was built between 1864 and 1867. The complex with a pond full of water lilies and lotus plants is located 7 km/4.4 mi from Hue. He spent a lot of time here, devoting hours to poetry, chess and fishing.

At the point where the two rivers, the Ta Trach and the Huu Trach merge to form the Perfume River, some 12 km/7.5 mi from Hue, is the Tomb of Emperor *Minh Mang*. Work (1840–43) started on it after his death. Palace, pavilion and three gateways were built in a park around two lakes, evoking a sense of space and peace.

Emperor *Khai Dinh's* tomb was built on Mount Chau between 1920 and 1931. Look carefully and you will see a fusion of Asian and European decorative features, testament to the emperor's interest in European culture, the multi-colour ceramic mosaics inside the temple add to the beauty and grace. The tombs of *Gia Long*, *Thieu Tri* and *Dong Khanh* are smaller and more modest.

Many organised tours include the tombs in their itinerary, so, to avoid the crowds, it is better to arrange your own tour in a hired boat along the Perfume River (*2 hours, including the Thien Mu Pagoda and Tomb of Minh Mang,*

19th century pavilion with the burial stele for Emperor Tu Duc

approx. 260,000 dong), possibly including a taxi. As the tombs are some distance apart, hire a private boat and put a cycle on board. It only costs approx. 26,000 dong per day to hire one and you will find cycle hire outlets everywhere. But do check that the brakes are working properly! The immediate vicinity of the tombs can get very crowded, so try to make your visit early in the morning or early evening. *In summer daily 6.30am–5.30pm, otherwise 7am–5pm | admission to each tomb approx. 104,000 dong (always check your change!)*

SAIGON AND THE SOUTH

Early in the morning is best, as the sun rises above the haze of the river delta – the Mekong, the vital artery of the south, where the nine arms or "nine dragons" flow into the sea.

Vietnam is waking up as the boats' engines chug on – fishermen in Chau Doc feed the catfish in the fish farms, in the Can Tho rice noodle factory, the diesel-powered mixers rotate at full speed. On Cai Rang market, not just fruit and vegetables, but also cable and incense sticks, change hands – from boat to boat.

Interestingly, here in the bustling Mekong Delta, there always used to be fewer roadside posters with socialist party slogans – in contrast to the once hard-line communist north. "Capital-ist" ways could never disappear here. Because in the end, it's a fact: Hanoi is a long way off. Now Saigon and the surrounding region is the engine behind a second, quiet, but very visible revolution. It's happening in the urban smart-set, among a small, wealthy upper strata. But also in the rapidly growing middle class, which toils away industriously day and night. At first sight Saigon today is like a wasps' nest. Constantly on the move, unsettling and at the same time exhilarating.

If you're relaxing on the powder-white beaches of Nha Trang, Phan Thiet/Mui Ne or on Phu Quoc Island, then it would be easy to imagine you were in the Caribbean, so stunningly beautiful are the holiday havens with their beautiful

The land of a thousand waterways – life pulsates along the Saigon River, and the Mekong Delta is Vietnam's rice bowl

beaches, shady coconut palms and a crystal-clear sea. Laissez-faire and a typically tropical magic – that is the south of Vietnam.

CAN THO

(140 C4) (*∅ E13*) **Long-tail boats, so called because of their outboard motor with an elongated propeller, which sweeps through the water like a whisk, shuttle back and forth along the countless canals and meandering waterways.**

The boatmen navigate their wooden craft with extraordinary skill often along very narrow channels – but their homes and stilt houses are far away from the main river. If you would like to explore the Mekong Delta off the beaten track, then you would be well advised to find accommodation in one of the hotels in this half-million strong city, which forms the political, commercial and cultural centre of the delta.

SIGHTSEEING

CAI RANG FLOATING MARKET ★ ●

The most attractive of the so-called "floating markets" in the Mekong Delta: Every morning, countless rowing boats or long-tail boats heavily laden with melons and pineapples, cucumbers and soup saucepans congregate near the Da Sau bridge (approx. 6 km/3.7 mi from the city

ways full. Huge selection of seafood, Chinese, Indian and Vietnamese classics such as spring rolls and hot pots, some Western (French) dishes and an excellent ice-cream menu. There are also a number of inexpensive food stalls on the banks of the river. *50 Hai Ba Trung | Ninh Khieu pier on the promenade near the night market | tel. 0292 3 81 56 16 | Moderate*

Shopping for early risers: stall at Cai Rang floating market

centre). It's enthralling to watch the lively market scene – if you want to watch the whole spectacle from the water, then hire a boat from the centre of Can Tho near the market *(approx. 260,000 dong for 2 hours)*. Get up early: It all gets going at sunrise and goes on until about 8am; by 9am activity is starting to tail off.

FOOD & DRINK

SAO HOM

A popular restaurant in the old market hall at a nice spot by the river, nearly al-

ENTERTAINMENT

How about a trip on the Hau Giang River? Noisy three- or four-storey *restaurant and disco vessels*, adorned with strings of flashing lights, are leaving daily at 6pm and 8pm from Ninh Kieu Park promenade. But perhaps – like the Vietnamese – you enjoy this brash and garish nightlife. It's a bit of Las Vegas in the Mekong Delta. Or you can enjoy an evening stroll on the new, enormous *Ninh Kieu pedestrian bridge* in the bright lights as far as Cai Khe Island.

WHERE TO STAY

KIM THO HOTEL

Take a ☀ INSIDER TIP room on the 8th floor or higher at this modern hotel and you will get the added bonus of a fine view. It's a riverside hotel and so can be a little noisy, but the smart parquet floors, large bathrooms, a daily share of vitamin C (fruit plate) and an elegant roof bar more than compensate. *51 rooms | 1a Ngo Gia Tu | tel. 0292 3 81 75 17 | www.kimtho.com | Budget–Moderate*

INSIDER TIP MEKONG LODGE

A river oasis with clean, thatched-roof cottages on the river bank, mosquito nets and outdoor bath, bicycle tours. Cookery courses are complimentary. What to pack: earplugs (because of the cargo boats underway early in the morning) and mosquito repellent. *30 rooms | An Hoa | Dong Hoa Hiep | Cai Be | approx. 80 km/49.7 mi outside Can Tho halfway to My Tho | mobile 091 8 53 10 38 (Mr Tuyen) | tel. in Saigon 028 39 95 20 87 | www.mekonglodge.com | Moderate*

VICTORIA CAN THO RESORT

Even if you're not staying here, you can still treat yourself to a sundowner on the ☀ terrace. Get superb views of the river or the tropical garden from the rooms of this colonial-inspired hotel. Plenty of recreational options and a Kids Corner. *92 rooms | Cai Khe Peninsula | free hotline tel. 18 00 59 99 55 | www.victoria hotels.asia | Expensive*

INFORMATION

Can Tho Tourist (20 Hai Ba Trung | tel. 0292 3 82 18 52 | www.canthotourist.com.vn)

CHAU DOC

(140 B4) (ⵔ D12) Everyday life in this city (pop. 200,000) by the Cambodian border still proceeds at a leisurely pace. Long-tail boats chug sedately along the Hau Giang River, children jump into the water from the decks of house boats, which float on empty oil drums. Many houseboats have nets slung beneath

---

★ **Cai Rang floating market**
Doing business on water – in Can Tho → p. 78

★ **Nha Trang**
Beach resort and tourist hang-out – a fusion of Nice and Ibiza by the South China Sea → p. 82

★ **Mui Ne**
A paradise for beach walkers and surfers → p. 85

★ **Phu Quoc**
Beach and ocean sunsets on Vietnam's biggest island → p. 87

★ **Chua Ngoc Hoang**
Heaven and hell in close proximity in Saigon's main temple → p. 91

★ **History Museum**
Track down some long forgotten civilisations in Saigon → p. 92

★ **Cho Lon**
Vibrant Chinatown in Saigon → p. 90

★ **Boat tour of the Mekong Delta**
Take a tour on the mighty river – you can't leave Vietnam without a meander through the delta → p. 100

★ **Cao Dai Temple**
Multi-colour architecture in Tay Ninh → p. 101

The towers of the Po Nagar Temple in Nha Trang are a testament to the heyday of Cham culture

Hon Chong Bay – the great jungle-like breakfast terrace alone is worth a detour.

NHA TRANG

(141 F2) (∅ H11) The coastal town of ★ Nha Trang has grown into a busy tourist centre with a growing skyline.
A wild fusion of Nice and Ibiza, including bonfire parties and fire shows, go go girls, shishas and pool bars.

Situated in a broad bay on the South China Sea, the city (pop. 450,000) is bordered to the north by the small Hon Son mountain range. Offshore are a number of green islands, which look the perfect place for dreamy afternoons lounging beneath palm trees.

The Tran Phu waterfront seems to go on forever, in fact it follows the beach for more than 5 km/3.1 mi. It ends in the south at the fishing harbour of Cau Da.

SIGHTSEEING

LONG SON PAGODA ꙮ
A *chua* built in honour of Kim Than Phat To, the white Buddha, who sits in a highly visible position to its rear. Some 152 stone steps lead up from Long Son, past a huge reclining Buddha. The pagoda itself was built in the late 19th century. Look out for the brightly-coloured dragons wrapped around the pillars either side of the main altar. *Thai Nguyen | approx. 500 m/1,640 ft west of the station*

PO NAGAR ꙮ
The Po Nagar Cham temple on a hill in the north of town has become a symbol for Nha Trang. Consisting of four towers, it was probably built between the 9th and 13th century. It is dedicated to Po Ino Nagar, the goddess who watches over the city and an incarnation of Shiva's spouse (Durga, also Parvati), the

divine mother. From the pagoda complex, there is a fine view over the harbour and its brightly painted fishing boats. *Daily 6am–6pm | admission approx. 26,000 dong*

FOOD & DRINK

INSIDER TIP **NHA TRANG VIEW** ⠧
Don't be put off by the price – here, the kilo counts! It's best to work up a good appetite or arrive in a family group at the romantic seafood restaurant and café. It's situated off the "party mile" just before the bridge over the bay and offers a fantastic (night-time) panorama of the coastal metropolis. You choose the seafood fresh from the sea water tanks. *Lau Ong Tu | north end of Tran Phu | mobile tel. 090 5 12 06 68 | www.nhatrangview. com.vn | Budget–Moderate*

SAILING CLUB – SANDALS RESTAURANT
Dimly-lit garden and beach restaurant, but also a popular disco club. From 10pm onwards, it's crowded, loud and hot (camp-fire). International crossover dishes, plus lots of cocktails. You just have to see it! *72–74 Tran Phu | tel. 0258 3 52 46 28 | www.sailingclubnhatrang. com | Expensive*

LEISURE, SPORTS & BEACH

ISLAND TOURS
Boat tours to the offshore islands are very popular. When booking a tour, don't be too thrifty and ask other travellers about their experiences with the various travel agencies such as *Jungle Travel (32 Tran Quang Khai | www.vietnamjungle travel.com)*.
A *cable car* crosses the sea to *Hon Tre (daily 8am–10pm | approx. 572,000 dong, including the admission for the Vinpearl amusement park)*.

BEACH
The 6 km/3.7 mi long, broad Nha Trang Beach is lined almost entirely with coconut palms. Hire a lounger and enjoy a relaxing day in the sun.

DIVING
Rainbow Divers (Rainbow Bar | 90a Hung Vuong | tel. 0258 3 52 43 51 | 24 hr hotline/mobile 09 08 78 17 56 | www.dive vietnam.com) is the leading diving operator in Vietnam and also offers courses in Nha Trang.

ENTERTAINMENT

Ibiza-style beach parties are popular events. Someone somewhere lights a

The perfect place to relax – Nha Trang Beach

A brick-red landscape – a walk along the Red Sand Canyon

what is considered to be a low rainfall region, the resorts attract an international band of windsurfers throughout almost the entire year. The best times for surfing are September/October to December, for kite surfing November to March/April. www.windsurf-vietnam.com

HIKING
One popular walk (it takes about one hour) starts near the village of *Ham Tien* and follows a creek through the dunes and past the bright red rock walls of the small *Red Sand Canyon* as far as the cascading source of the *Suoi Tien (Fairy Springs)*.

ENTERTAINMENT

JIBE'S
Where the surfers meet up in the evening – in the middle of the beach. *90 Nguyen Dinh Chieu | km 13 marker | www.windsurf-vietnam.com*

MIA MUI NE
Lifestyle club for the smart set with the excellent *Sandals Restaurant* (fusion food, *Expensive*), plus upmarket ● beach bar serving great cocktails. *24 Nguyen Dinh Chieu | Ham Tien | www.miamuine.com*

WHERE TO STAY

CHAM VILLAS
An excellent spot on Mui Ne – stylishly-decorated bungalows with palm-leaf roofs, four poster beds, lush greenery and a giant pool await the guests. *18 bungalows | 32 Nguyen Dinh Chieu | Ham Tien | tel. 0252 3 74 12 34 | www.chamvillas.com | Expensive*

COCO BEACH RESORT
One of the nicest bungalow villages on the beach – stilt houses and villas (no TV, but air-conditioned) dotted around by the beach and in the garden. There are also two very good restaurants and a small pool. *34 bungalows | 58 Nguyen Dinh Chieu | km 12.5 marker | Ham Tien | tel. 0252 3 84 71 11 | www.cocobeach.net | Expensive*

FULL MOON BEACH RESORT
Pretty, timber bungalows, rooms with four-poster beds and pink-tiled bathrooms. Where the surfing set stay. *27 rooms | km 13.5 marker | Ham Tien | tel. 0252 3 84 70 08 | fullmoonbeach.com.vn | Moderate*

INSIDER TIP HIEP HOA RESORT
Small, but beautiful: here you almost roll out of bed into the sea – or the pool. And

for a very reasonable price in this pleasant Vietnamese family guesthouse, one of the last on this booming beach! Tightly-packed blue chalets and a two-storey building; the rows of chalets have fans or air conditioning and terrace or balcony overlooking the shady gardens or palm beach. *15 rooms | 80 Nguyen Dinh Chieu | tel. 0252 3 84 72 62 | Budget*

MIA RESORT

Pretty complex, rooms with French balconies, Australian management. *31 rooms | 24 Nguyen Dinh Chieu | Ham Tien | tel. 0252 3 84 74 40 | www.miamuine.com | Moderate–Expensive*

WHERE TO GO

TA CU ♨ (141 E3) (𝄞 G11)

On the 694 m/2,277 ft high Ta Cu (also known as Ta Ku) in the nature reserve of the same name is probably the tallest Buddha statue in Vietnam. The Sakyamuni Buddha measures a total of 49 m/160.8 ft from the tips of his toes to the top of his enlightened head. To reach the statue involves either a 2-hour hike through the woods, or – more comfortably – a 10-minute cable-car ride. At the top pilgrims and visitors are welcomed to the over 150-year-old *Linh Son Truong Tho* monastery *(daily 7am–5pm | admission including cable car approx. 234,000 dong | approx. 30 km/28.6 mi south-west of Phan Thiet near Ham Thuan Nam)*

PHU QUOC

(140 A4) (𝄞 C–D12–13) ★ When you make holiday on Vietnam's largest island, you're already close to the Cambodian border.
The plots for countless luxury resorts have already been earmarked (unfortunately currently many are still building sites). Awaiting exploration, mainly on the south coast, are some 40 km/24.9 mi of beaches fringed with coconut palms against a jungle backdrop. A 27-hole golf course (Vinpearl Hotel) has already opened and three other golf courses are planned as well as a cruise ship terminal and a casino. A cable car 8 km/5 mi across the sea connects with the neighbouring island of Hon Thom – with concrete pillars protruding skywards, ten times higher than the coconut palms. Phu Quoc (pop. 90,000) with its capital city Duong Dong is said to be Vietnam's answer to Phuket, with

LOW BUDGET

The INSIDER TIP *Town House 50* **(U C4) (𝄞 c4)** *(12 rooms | 50e Bui Thi Xuan | tel. 028 39 25 02 10)* in Saigon offers modern rooms (WiFi, lovely baths) and a bountiful breakfast with lots of fresh fruit. The ultra-stylish *Town House 23* **(U D4) (𝄞 d4)** *(23 Dang Thi Nhu | tel. 028 39 15 14 91)* also has a dorm room. From approx. 208,000 dong, double rooms from 676,000 dong. *www.townhousesaigon.com*

At the open-air restaurant *Lac Canh (44 Nguyen Binh Khiem | tel. 0258 3 82 13 91)* in Nha Trang they serve seafood (from 52,000 dong), chicken, BBQ beef (from 65,000 dong).

At the *Dinh Cau Night Market (Vo Thi Sau)* in Duong Dong, Phu Quoc's island capital, you can get fresh seafood and fish (hot pots, king prawns, cattlefish...) daily from 5pm for 52,000–78,000 dong.

Large pool, French cuisine in a colonial-style restaurant. *70 rooms | Bai Truong | tel. 0297 3 98 29 88 | www.sofitel.com | Expensive*

INFORMATION

Information in all hotels and travel agencies and on www.phuquocislandguide.com

SAIGON (HO CHI MINH CITY)

 MAP INSIDE THE BACK COVER **(140 C3) (*m* E–F12) Saigon, with a population of around 9 million, is the old and the new power base for the Republic of Vietnam – and offers an intriguing journey through time between colonial sites, food stalls and skyscrapers.**

Vietnam's largest city, divided into 19 districts *(quan)*, has successfully retained much of its charm from the French colonial period. Right next to it you can see how the Saigon of today looks: millions of mopeds, cyclos and pedestrians fight for space between trucks and buses – the result is generally a noisy and chaotic free-for-all.

But right in the middle of it all you will find colourful, incense-clouded temples and pagodas and also markets such as Binh Tay in Saigon's "Chinatown", the western district of ★ *Cho Lon*. Cho Lon ("big market") used to be a separate settlement, where refugees from southern China settled here about 300 years ago and started trading, and that is precisely what their descendants still do – on the pavements, in the narrow alleys and in the multi-storey market hall.

A ● journey by cyclo is an experience. Somehow your "driver" manages to negotiate what you would regard as traffic mayhem (tip: only book the organised tours via the hotel or a travel agency).

Fancy a nice view? Then head to the 265 m/869 ft high ☆ *Bitexco Financial Tower* (U E4) (*m* e4) (*daily 9.30am–9.30pm | admission observation deck on the 49th floor approx. 208,000 dong | between Ngo Duc Ke and Hai Trieu | www.bitexcofinancialtower.com)* with 68 floors, shops, a helicopter pad and a café on the 50th floor.

SIGHTSEEING

OLD OPERA HOUSE/CITY THEATRE
(U E3) (*m* e3)

A sight for sore eyes, not only because of the two angels sitting above the entrance. The building, which dates from the start of the 20th century, was used post-1956 as an assembly hall for part of the South Vietnamese parliament. In 1975, it was re-opened as a theatre, and renamed Saigon Concert Hall. The touristy but artistic show is funny and well worth seeing *(Mon–Fri 6pm, Sat/Sun also 8pm | admission from approx. 598,000 dong)*. It features acrobat bars, bamboo bridges and coracles. *Dong Khoi/corner of Le Loi | information at the box office and on www.luneproduction.com*

CHUA GIAC LAM (0) (*m* 0)

From the outside, the Chua Giac Lam is rather unspectacular, but has experienced much: the oldest pagoda of Saigon was built in 1744 and is considered one of the most magnificent in town. Ten monks live in the building, which reflects Taoist and Confucian influences. The most striking features are the 118 gilded wooden statues (including various portrayals of Buddha), the

Saigon up high: the view of the skyline with the Bitexco Financial Tower from the roof of the AB Tower

ornate carvings on the altar and on the 98 pillars in the main hall. *118 Lac Long Quan | 3 km/1.9 mi north-west of Cho Lon*

CHUA NGOC HOANG ★ ●
(U D1) *(🗺 d1)*
You should visit Saigon's most important pagoda where heaven and hell are

---

CITY WHERE TO START?
Get a moped taxi, cyclo or taxi to **Notre Dame Cathedral (U D3)** *(🗺 d3)*, where you can start your walk. Situated on Dong Khoi shopping boulevard (Rue Catinat in colonial days) are the classic hotels, such as the Continental or the Majestic. Carry on past the General Post Office and the old Opera House as far as the river promenade. Or get a first overview of the city from the **Bitexco Financial Tower (U E4)** *(🗺 e4)*.

---

alongside each other. It's also practical on earth: if you only light enough incense sticks, it might also work out with reincarnation, offspring or a lottery win … Here, the Vietnamese worship Ngoc Hoang, the powerful Jade emperor of Taoism. The main entrance flanked by guardian figures leads first to a Buddhist altar. Only then do you arrive in the main hall with the statue of the Jade Emperor, surrounded by his ministers Bac Dau and Nam Tao, plus four guardians. The Chief of Hell, Thanh Hoang, dominates the side room to the left of the altar. Easy to miss is the small Than Tai, the god of finances dressed all in white. The Torments of the Ten Hells are shown on wooden panels. But heaven is not far away. The small, usually smoke-filled room on the right attracts many parents and childless couples. Here twelve celestial women clad in precious silk give support to women hoping to conceive. *73 Mai Thi Luu | north of the city centre* between silk clothing and lacquerware in Dong Khoi – rather expensive, e.g. at *Khai Silk (no. 107)*, Hai Ba Trung, Le Loi and Nguyen Van Troi (galleries) (all (U D–E3) *(Ⓜ d–e3)*). Armani and Gucci, a great food market, plus games rooms for the youngsters in the ● *Vincom Center* (U E3) *(Ⓜ e3) (70 Le Thanh Ton)*. Antiques and Buddhas in all shapes and sizes in Le Cong Kieu, the second-hand dealers' street (try the *Ngoc Bich family* (U D4) *(Ⓜ d4) (no. 64)*.

Cheap and cheerful imitations, DVDs and T-shirts are available in the *Saigon Square 1* department store (U D3) *(Ⓜ d3) (Nam Ky Khoi Nghia | near Ben Thanh market)* and *Saigon Square 3* (U D2) *(Ⓜ d2) (Hai Ba Trung)*. Alternatively, barge through the crowds in the 100-year-old *Ben Thanh market* (U D4) *(Ⓜ d4) (daily 6am–6pm | Le Loi | www.ben-thanh-market.com)* (do haggle at least 30–50 per cent, unfortunately there are many pickpockets! In the evening night market with food stalls). Slightly cheaper are the wholesale *Binh Tay Market* (currently being restored) in Cho Lon, the *An Dong Market* (U B5) *(Ⓜ b5) (An Duong Vuong)* (Saigon's largest market), the *Nguyen Dinh Chieu Market* (0) *(Ⓜ 0)* (1 Le Tu Tai) (an outdoor market with everything from clothes to gold to teas) and the streets around the backpackers' row Pham Ngu Lao (U C–D4) *(Ⓜ c–d4)*, such as the "Painting Streets" Tran Phu and Bui Vien, are where you can pick up fake masterpieces!

Near the *Hardrock Cafe (39 Le Duan)* you can wander around the quiet little streets, past cafés and stands with books and souvenirs.

AUTHENTIQUE HOME

Pretty decor and artistic and practical items for the living room back home: wonderful hand-painted cups and vases, wall carpets, embroidered cushions, bags etc. – not exactly cheap, but these are not mass-produced merchandise. Pottery and ceramic workshops are also offered. *Two shops* (U E3) *(Ⓜ e3): 71/1 Mac Thi Buoi and 113 Le Thanh Ton | www.authentiquehome.com*

THE HOUSE OF SAIGON
(U D4) *(Ⓜ d4)*

Lots of colourful items: here, you'll be sure to find something – flip-flops and handbags, tea or coffee, oils and soaps, ceramics or silk dresses. *258 Le Thanh Ton | www.thehouseofsaigon.com*

MEKONG CREATIONS (U D4) *(Ⓜ d4)*

Here there are beautiful souvenirs, also made of rattan, papier mâché or bamboo. The hats, scarves, bags, textiles, clothing and quilts are created by women with disabilities who previously earned about £11.50/US$15 per month, but now earn four times as much working for this initiative. *68 Le Loi | near Ben Thanh market | www.mekong-plus.com*

LEISURE & WELLBEING

Trails of Indochina (33 Le Trung Nghia | tel. 028 38 11 33 88 | www.trailsofindochina.com): Tours of Indochina.
XO Tours (mobile tel. 093 3 08 37 27 | www.xotours.vn): hop on the moped! Drivers in Ao Dai dress collect you, even with "bodyguards" and accident insurance, e.g. to depart on a *Foodie Tour.*

LA MAISON L'APOTHIQUAIRE SPA ●
(U D3) *(Ⓜ d3)*

One of the best day spas in town pampers its guests in an old villa (pick-up service). *Daily 9am–8pm | 64a Truong Dinh | tel. 028 39 32 51 81 | www.spasaigon.com*

ENTERTAINMENT

INSIDER TIP ▶ CARMEN BAR
(U E3) (🏥 e3)

Loud, cool and: smoke-filled! But it's still an absolutely fun and brilliant location with unbeatable atmosphere and diversi-

QUI CUISINE MIXOLOGY
(U E2) (🏥 e2)

Whatever your choice – well-chilled wine, champagne or cocktails – the bartenders know what they're doing. The food is also tempting – and fairly pricey. *22 Le Thanh Ton | www.quilounge.com*

An alternative to fake Rembrandts: propaganda posters have become popular souvenirs

ty. Live bands, predominantly Latino and Flamenco sounds in this dimly-lit setting, plus cocktails, beer, wine, whisky. Packed to the rafters at weekends. *8 Ly Tu Trong*

GLOW SKYBAR (U D3) (🏥 D3)

You must see at least one sky bar in Saigon! As the *Chill SaiGon Skybar* is now overcrowded with a trendy public (and it's particularly pricey), you can happily switch to the slightly quieter sky bar to enjoy a sundowner or nightcap and admire the glinting night skyline from here. On weekends, it's best to reserve one of the illuminated high tables! *93 Nguyen Du | in the President Place building | www.glowsaigon.vn*

REPUBLIC CLUB (U C4) (🏥 c4)

If your ears are still ringing from the party three days later, then you were in Saigon and most probably in the popular Republic in the heart of the backpackers' district. Motto: "In fun we trust" and "dress to impress"!

So, don your high heels, and enjoy the vibe and cocktails. *19 Do Quang Dao | www.republicclub.vn*

SAX 'N' ART CLUB (U D3) (🏥 d3)

Small and friendly jazz club run by saxophonist Tran Manh Tuan. Large screen and jazz videos to watch while sipping cocktails, until the live bands get started from 9pm. Happy Hour 5pm–8pm. *28 Le Loi*

WATER PUPPET THEATRE
(U D3) (*m d3*)

The *Rong Vang Golden Dragon Water Puppet Theatre* is a fine example of the genre, 200 seats *(performances daily 5pm and 6.30pm | admission approx. 234,000 dong | 55b Nguyen Thi Minh Khai | tel. 028 39 30 21 96)*. Water puppet theatre also during the day in the *History Museum* (see p. 92).

WHERE TO STAY

In *Pham Ngu Lao street* (U C–D4) (*m c–d4)*, a district with guest houses, cafes and bars, travel agencies, banks, tailors and souvenir shops etc. has evolved. There really is nowhere else in the country where you will find such good and inexpensive accommodation as here. The central *Thi Sach* street has seen a lot of very good, new hotels open, many of which are in the mid-range, business category, i.e. the *May Hotel* (U E3) (*m e3) (118 rooms | 28–30 Duong Thich Sach | tel. 028 38 23 45 01 | www.mayhotel. com.vn | Moderate)* with a covered rooftop pool.

HOTEL CONTINENTAL ● (U E3) (*m e3*)
Evidence of the big wide world can be found in Saigon's oldest hotel, which dates from 1885. Famous literary figures, such as Somerset Maugham and Graham Greene, stayed in this grand hotel. Pretty courtyard. *87 rooms | 132–134 Dong Khoi | tel. 028 38 29 92 01 | www.continental saigon.com | Expensive*

MERAKI BOUTIQUE HOTEL
(U C4) (*m c4*)

Friendly guest house in the travellers' quarter and partyzone; with lift. Tiny rooms with IDD, TV, WiFi, refrigerator, some with balcony. Breakfast is served on the roof terrace, even late – if you want to party, this is the ideal address! Especially beautiful (and quiet) is the almost completely glassy attic rooms, the INSIDERTIP Rooftop Suite *(Moderate)*. *19 rooms | 178 Bui Vien | near Pham Ngu Lao | tel. 028 38 38 53 37 | www.meraki hotel.com | Budget*

INSIDERTIP MS. YANG 1+2
(U C4) (*m c4*)

At this homestay your accommodation is about 20 minutes' walk from the centre of the old town. Two friendly sisters have plenty of tips for travelling off the beaten track. Four, simply furnished (balcony) rooms have air-conditioning, WIFI and a shower bath. The day starts with traditional food like noodle soup. People get up early in this quarter – take some earplugs with you ... *4 rooms | mobile tel. 0120 3 40 73 48 | msyanghomestay@ gmail.com | Budget*

PRINCE SAIGON (U E4) (*m e4*)
In the heart of the city; rooms on the upper floors are the quietest; giant buffet breakfast, small pool, nice piano bar in the lobby. *198 rooms | 63 Nguyen Hue | tel. 028 38 22 29 99 | www.saigonprince hotel.com | Moderate–Expensive*

THIEN XUAN HOTEL (U D4) (*m d4*)
Nice rooms, stucco ceilings, some with balcony (rooms at the front are noisy), friendly and professional service. *68 rooms | 108–110 Le Thanh Ton | near Ben Thanh market | tel. 028 38 22 91 60 | www.thienxuanhotel.com.vn | Budget–Moderate*

VILLA SONG SAIGON (0) (*m 0*)
A true oasis in colonial-style, located outside the city centre, but directly on the river; just ten minutes from town with the free shuttle bus. Pool in the garden, a good restaurant and a small spa.

Pedestrians, cycles, mopeds – traffic chaos in Saigon

23 rooms | 197/2 Nguyen Van Huong | Thao Dien district | tel. 028 37 44 60 90 | www.villasong.com | Expensive

INFORMATION

Tourist information in the General Post Office (125 Dong Khoi | opposite the cathedral)

WHERE TO GO

INSIDER TIP **CAT TIEN NATIONAL PARK** (141 D3) (*ω F11*)

If you go exploring here, with a little luck, you will see – and hear – the endangered yellow-cheeked gibbons: they are famous for their early-morning duet choruses, and you're guaranteed to get goose bumps! The park is also one of the last refuges of the Indochinese tiger; plus, there are also clouded leopards and the Gaur, a wild cattle species – but you usually won't see them when you tour the park because they hide in the jungle (if they haven't fallen prey to poachers).

A visit to the British-run 🐵 *Primate Center* is also worthwhile, as is a stop at the 🐵 *reintroduction project for Asian black bears and wild cats (www.go-east.org)* and the "Gibbon Trek" (from 4.40am). Plus, some 360 bird species have been counted in the park! You can go on an exploratory tour with a guide (book at least four days in advance), for which a charge of about 520,000 dong per day is made, or race the trails on a hire bike (check it beforehand). Basic overnight accommodation (*Budget, electricity only until 6pm, bring a torch!*) is available at the park entrance. *Admission approx. 182,000 dong | information from the National Park Service (office in Than Phu at the bus stop, 24 km/14.9 mi from the National Park | tel. 0251 3 66 92 28 | www.namcattien.org)*

CON DAO (140 C3) (*ω F14*)

The Con Dao archipelago, which consists of 16 islands in the South China Sea, is slowly but surely becoming a holiday destination. The mountainous main

DISCOVERY TOURS

① VIETNAM AT A GLANCE

START: ① Saigon END: ⑫ Hanoi	**21 days** Driving time (without stops) **30 hours**
Distance: ➡ approx. 1,900 km/1,181 mi	

COSTS: approx. 46,800,000 dong (approx. 26,000,000 dong for car/driver/petrol plus approx. 20,800,000 dong per person for accommodation, food & drink and admission fees)

WHAT TO PACK: swim gear, hiking boots, raincoat, sun protection

IMPORTANT TIPS: options for car bookings: *Trails of Indochina* (tel. 028 38 44 10 05 | *www.trailsofindochina.com*); *Handspan* (tel. 024 39 26 28 28 | *www.handspan.com*); *Exotic Voyages* (free hotline 001 888 4 79 00 68 | *www.exoticvoyages.com*)

If you do not want to visit the ⑩ **Phong Nha Cave**, you can save time by flying north from Hue and then continuing the route.

Would you like to explore the places that are unique to this country? Then the Discovery Tours are just the thing for you – they include terrific tips for stops worth making, breathtaking places to visit, selected restaurants and fun activities. It's even easier with the Touring App: download the tour with map and route to your smartphone using the QR Code on pages 2/3 or from the website address in the footer below – and you'll never get lost again even when you're offline.

TOURING APP

→ p. 2/3

This route along the coast from south to north stops at historically significant sites and great places to swim. Take in some of Vietnam's most beautiful areas such as the dry Ha Long Bay with its fairy-tale mountains and experience the adventure of exploring the fascinating Phong Nha Cave.

Breathe in the city air of ❶ **Saigon** → **p. 90** to kick-off this tour. Explore the bustling "Chinatown" **Cho Lon**, go for a "walk" with a cylco and visit the Jade Emperor in his pagoda **Chua Ngoc Hoang**. Then head to the **Glow Skybar** for a sundowner and a view of the skyline.

DAY 1–2

❶ Saigon

❸ Ha Long City

25 km/15.5 mi

❹ Ha Long Bay → p. 35

25 km/15.5 mi

❺ Ha Long City

Drive further along the N5. Shortly before Hai Phong, turn off towards ❸ Ha Long City. The city has three piers by now: **Bai Chay**, **Hon Gai** and the Marina on **Tuan Chau Island**; there are departure points for a **two-day boat trip through the breathtaking ❹ Ha Long Bay** → p. 35 (two nights on board). When you first see the 2,000 or so towering limestone rocks, you might just start to believe in the legend of the "descending dragon" *(ha long)*.

A real challenge: rock climbing on Cat Ba

Shortly after setting sail, you will fall prey to the charm of this island world. There is hardly a rock that hasn't been given a special name that somehow reflects its shape. You'll have no troubling figuring out which one is "Camel Island" or "Turtle Island". Jump into a kayak (from the boat down a ladder or on more exclusive tours directly on the beach) for an hour or two to paddle through hidden lagoons and floating villages. After these maritime adventures head back to **❺ Ha Long City** or Tuan Chau Island.

Are you up for an even greater physical challenge in this fantastic scenery of Ha Long Bay? Get out your climbing gear and head to the steep cliffs of Cat Ba → p. 39, a national park island that, along with the adjacent Lan Ha Bay → p. 117, is a true paradise for rock climbers!

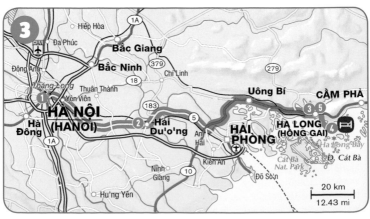

④ MANGROVES, A NATIONAL PARK AND THE COASTAL ROAD

START: ① Can Gio END: ⑪ Nha Trang	5 days Driving time (without stops) 15 hours
Distance: ➡ approx. 700 km/435 mi	

COSTS: approx. 11,960,000 dong (6,500,000 dong for car/driver/petrol; 5,460,000 dong per person for accommodation, food & drink and admission fees)

WHAT TO PACK: swim gear, hiking boots, binoculars, torch, raincoat, sun protection, leech socks, mosquito repellent/protective clothing (malaria area!)

IMPORTANT TIPS: it is best to plan this tour for the dry season from Nov/Dec until March/April.
Car hire, e. g. with *VN Rent a car (www.vnrentacar.com)*
③ Cat Tien National Park: make reservations at least four days in advance and book a guide *(www.namcattien.org)*!

Follow this route from the Biosphere Reserve of Can Gio near Saigon to the teeming jungles in Cat Tien National Park, and then head up into the more temperate highlands near Da Lat before returning to the coast at Nha Trang via a stunning mountain pass. Nature, great views and fantastic swims are all part of this tour.

The tour sets off 55 km/34.2 mi south-east of Saigon in the alluvial sand of the "island" ① **Can Gio** (approx. 309 mi²) formed by the Saigon River that is famous for its mangrove forest. Although largely destroyed by the Agent Orange defoliant used by the US military in the Vietnam War, the forest with its trees atop buttress roots has once again become a haven for many species of fish, reptiles (e.g. monitor lizards) and birds. It is even home to a Macaque colony. Try to get an early start, around 8am if you can, for a two-hour tandem kayak tour in order to avoid the busloads of tourists.

Drive towards Saigon and turn onto the N 1 heading north-east. After the industrial town of Bien Hoa, at km 69 in Dau Giay, follow the N 20 as it branches off towards the mountains, passing rubber plantations and fruit trees. Many fishermen live on houseboats and in floating villages on the ② **Tri An Reservoir** (aka: La Nga Lake).

DAY 1–2

① Can Gio

135 km / 84 mi

② Tri An Reservoir

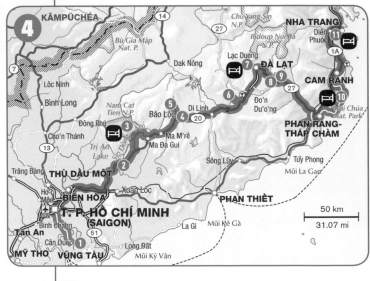

45 km/28 mi

❸ Cat Tien National Park

DAY 3

❹ Bao Loc
18 km/11.2 mi

❺ Dambri Waterfall
94 km/58.4 mi

❻ Pongour Waterfall

After about 70 km/43.5 mi near Phu Thanh, a track leads off to ❸ **Cat Tien National Park** → p. 99. Without a guide, you can hike for about three hours (approx. 5 km/3.1 mi, best after arriving in the evening) on a INSIDER TIP jungle trail to **Crocodile Lake**. Keep your eyes peeled for the different kinds of birds and, with a bit of luck, even some gibbons and Colobine monkeys. You can spend the night, e.g at Crocodile Lake in the **Green Bamboo Lodge** *(7 rooms, 5 tents | mobile 097 3 34 63 45 | www.greenbamboolodge.net | Budget)* or in the stylish, yet rustic **Forest Floor Lodge** *(8 rooms | tel. 0251 66 98 90 | www.forestfloorlodges.com | Expensive)*. Explore the national park in more depth the next day – this time accompanied by a guide.

Drive along the bumpy road back towards the N 20, crossing through Ma Da Gui (four-wheel drive is a must in the rainy season!). **The route slowly winds up to a height of 1,500 m/4,921 ft**, where a dense jungle surrounds the pass. You can see a few picturesque temple shrines and waterfalls on the wayside. **You will come to the plateau near the small town of** ❹ **Bao Loc** → p. 60, which is an ideal place to tour tea factories or silkworm farms. Check out the ❺ **Dambri Waterfall (near Bao Loc)** and the ❻ **Pongour Waterfall (near Duc Trong,**

48 km/29.8 mi south of Da Lat) – the waterfalls are the most spectacular at the end of the rainy season (November/December). Poster-clad walls and greenhouses herald your arrival in the mountain town of **⑦ Da Lat → p. 58**, a favourite destination among Vietnamese honeymooners.

Leave Da Lat heading eastward towards Phan Rang on the serpentine N 20 and turn left on the N 27 towards the coast. The route passes the **⑧ Da Nhim Reservoir** (aka: Don Duong Lake) and a huge hydroelectric power plant. The fascinating **⑨ Ngoan Muc Pass**, from which you can see the coast about 60 km/37.3 mi away if the weather is good, winds approx. 1,000 m/3,281 ft **down to the lowlands**, where palm trees and cacti abound. **A few kilometres before the coastal town of Phan Rang**, you will see the Cham temple Pо Klong Garai → p. 59 atop a hill and, approx. 15 km/9.3 mi south of Phan Rang, Po Rome.

Depart Phan Rang via the Coastal Highway 702 to the north. The road runs past fishing bays and pretty rock formations, sand dunes, gleaming white beaches and green hills. Luxury hotels with spectacular settings await along the way, e.g. **⑩ Amanoi Resort** (31 rooms | tel. 0259 3 77 07 77 | www.aman.com | *Expensive*) **in the amazingly beautiful Vinh Hy Bay**. The seaside restaurants built on stilts also offer plenty of refreshment.

The Coastal Highway 702 runs further north to Bing Tien near the harbour of Cam Ranh, which served as an American Navy base from 1964–73. **Drive a bit further north on the N 1 to the seaside resort of ⑪ Nha Trang → p. 82.** Spend a relaxing day at the beach to end this tour in true beach holiday style.

48 km/29.8 mi

⑦ Da Lat

DAY 4

⑧ Da Nhim Reservoir

5 km/3.1 mi

⑨ Ngoan Muc Pass

130 km/81 mi

⑩ Amanoi Resort

DAY 5

99 km/61.5 mi

⑪ Nha Trang

Short time out in the lively resort town Nha Trang

SPORTS & ACTIVITIES

The range of activity holidays in Vietnam is gradually widening. But don't expect perfection – some of the leisure pursuits, such as caving, are still new. Safety standards at some Vietnamese companies are still rudimentary. The cheaper the tour (kayaking or rock climbing, for example), the more inexperienced the guides are likely to be.

CAVING

Superlatives are not enough: this is the most beautiful, deepest, most adventurous, species-diverse and possibly the largest cave in the world! Keen cavers love exploring the 14 vast chambers in the **INSIDER TIP** *Phong Nha Cave (www.phongnhakebang.vn)*. It is loca-ted close to Son Trach, 55 km/34.2 mi north-west of Dong Hoi in central Vietnam. Caving tours to the cave are organised by **INSIDER TIP** *Phong Nha Farmstay (Cu Nam | Dong Hoi | tel. 052 3 67 51 35 | mobile 094 4 75 98 64 | phong-nha-cave.com | Budget–Moderate | tour approx. 780,000–7,800,000 dong)* (book well in advance!) together with tour operator Oxalis Adventures *(www.oxalis.com. vn)*. You can also visit the cave by boat *(several caves, admission to each approx. 234,000–442,000 dong per person, boat included)*. A tried-and-tested tour operator is *Footprint Vietnam Travel (30a Alley 12A | Ly Nam De | Hanoi | tel. 024 39 33 28 44 | www.footprint.vn)*. Very spectacular is the almost 9 km/5.6 mi long *Hang Son Doong Cave (www.sondoong*

Workouts for everyone: Active holiday enthusiasts will be breaking new ground in Vietnam, but they can still look forward to adventure

cave.org), which you can explore on a week-long, very demanding trekking tour (*US$3,000 | only 200 tourists with climbing experience permitted each year, long waiting list | www.oxalis.com.vn*).

CYCLING

For longer routes, cyclists should bring their own bike and also a good selection of spare parts. Good bikes (rental costs approx. 26,000 to 52,000 dong per day) are rare in Vietnam, as are bike shops with a good supply of spare parts. Favourite cycling areas include the flat Mekong Delta as well as trips around the cities of Hoi An, Hue and Tam Coc (Ha Long Bay on Land). Avoid the N 1 (heavy traffic, dangerous stretches). For some stretches, you can switch to the lovely coastal roads (e.g. the Coastal Highway 702 north of Phan Rang up to Nha Trang, approx. 100 km/62 mi) or the new Ho Chi Minh highway through the fantastic countryside (although it is sometimes quite mountainous and sparsely populated, which means that there is not much accommodation available). *Information: Footloose Adventure Travel | 3 Springs Pavement, Ilkley, West Yorkshire | tel. 00 44 1943 60 40 30 | www.footlooseadventure.co.uk | www.cyclingvietnam.net*

DIVING

Nha Trang, Phu Quoc, the coast off Hoi An and the Con Dao archipelago are the best sites in Vietnam for diving. Nha Trang ad Phu Quoc boast a number of diving schools. Visibility under water here is on average 10–15 m/32.8–49.2 ft, during the dry season up to 30 m/98.4 ft. Currently there are about 25 dive sites and an artificial wreck is planned. In addition to relatively well-preserved hard and soft corals, there are also tropical fish as well as sand sharks and oceanic white-tip sharks. Two dives (one tank each) cost from approx. 2,080,000 dong. Further information: *Rainbow Divers (www.divevietnam.com)*

GOLF

Golf is the latest craze in the "new Vietnam". There are several golf courses suitable for both professional and amateur players, such as the ones near Hanoi and Saigon, in Phan Thiet and in Da Lat. *www.kingsislandgolf.com, www.vietnamgolfresorts.com*

HIKING

The best areas for hiking are the Bach Ma National Park, the hilly area around Sa Pa, the Ba Be National Park as well as the highlands near Da Lat , e.g. Mount Lang Biang. You will need to bring your own equipment, e.g. boots, walking sticks, rucksack, water bottles, energy bars. You can buy high-quality trekking equipment in Saigon, Hanoi and Sa Pa. Recommended tour operator: *Phat Tire Ventures (9 Nguyen Van Troi | Da Lat | tel. 0263 3 82 94 22 | mobile 09 83 84 72 17 | www.ptv-vietnam.com)*.

KAYAK TOURS

By far the best is the sea kayak tour through Ha Long Bay. You can choose from tours of between 1 and 6 days in length, all with an English-speaking escort. Some 6–8 km/3.7–5 mi covered per day, depending on the fitness level of the group and number of caves to be visited. On multi-day tours, overnight stops in

Adventures on the water: Vietnam offers ideal conditions for paddling tours

tents; luxury offers include accommodation on a boat. Two-day tours including meals cost from around 5,200,000 dong per person; book through a reputable tour operator, e.g. *SeaCanoe and Inserimex Travel (www.johngray-seacanoe.com)*.

ROCK CLIMBING

Headfirst into the mostgorgeous scenery: INSIDER TIP► *Ha Long Bay and Lan Ha Bay* near Cat Ba are the perfect destinations for rock climbers. The views are terrific, the challenges great. But if you want to climb independently, you must bring your own equipment. You also need the experience of captains and guides, who know the tides, as access to many of the caves inside the giant limestone rocks is only possible when the water is at a certain level. Information and tours (with trained climbers and equipment): *Asia Outdoors (1/4 Street No. 229 | Cat Ba | tel. 0225 3 68 84 50 | www.asiaoutdoors.com.vn | day tours approx. 1,040,000 dong)*

SAILING & WINDSURFING

One excellent windsurfing beach is Mui Ne near Phan Thiet. Competitions such as the *Starboard Vietnam Fun Cup* are

staged here. For more information contact *Jibe's Club (Mui Ne | www.windsurf-vietnam.com)*. All the action starts in the *Full Moon Beach Resort (km 13.5 marker | Ham Tien | Mui Ne | tel. 0252 3 84 70 08 | www.fullmoonbeach.com.vn)*. A windsurfing package for three days, including half-board and board rental, costs around 7,800,000 dong. Leisure pursuits on offer at the *Mia Resort (24 Nguyen Dinh Chieu | Ham Tien | tel. 0252 3 84 74 40 | www.miamuine.com)* include surfing and kite surfing.

Vietnam's sailing scene likes to gather in the coastal resorts of Nha Trang and Mui Ne/Phan Tiet.

SPA TREATMENTS

With everything from scrubs or wraps to foot reflex massages and facials to Swedish and Thai massages, the pampered guests at the spas in Saigon and Hanoi feel like they are on cloud nine. Many beach hotels, especially in Da Nang, Hoi An and Qui Nhon, offer yoga with ocean views. In the hot springs and mud baths near Nha Trang (Thap Ba), Hue (Thanh Tan) and Binh Chau (near Vung Tau), you can enjoy mud pack treatments and thermal springs – wellness à la Vietnam!

TAI CHI

If you are interested in the Chinese martial art of tai chi (or *thai cuc quyen*) in Vietnamese, you will have to get up early. For the equivalent of a few pence, you can join courses in Saigon: Tue–Sat 5.30am–7am and 7am–8.30pm in *Le Van Tam Park (Hai Ba Trung/corner Dien Bien Phu)*, furthermore in the *Van Hoa Park (Nguyen Du)*, in *Tao Dam Cultural Park (approx. 8am–9am)* and in the *"23/9" park (Pham Ngu Lao)*. In Hanoi: by the *Hoan Kiem Lake* and in the *Botanical Garden*.

TRAVEL
WITH KIDS

All *tay* – Westerners – are made very welcome in Vietnam, but those travelling with their own children even more so. Children usually find there is plenty to keep them entertained. Children up to two years of age (or less than 80 cm/2.6 ft) can usually fly free of charge in Vietnam and, in many situations, children up to 10 years of age are granted a reduction of up to 50 percent, e.g. coach tours, excursions or amusement parks. Saigon and Hanoi and also Phan Thiet, Mui Ne and Nha Trang are well catered for holidaymakers and so make ideal bases for family vacations. The latter resort is very popular, because it has such beautiful, soft sandy beaches. Many hotel pools cater to the whole family and can be used by non-guests for a small daily fee (approx. 130,000 dong).

HANOI SUPER KARTING CENTRE
(0) *(𝖗 0)*
Always a winner with older children (and young-at-heart parents). Whiz around in a go-kart for approx. 78,000 dong. *Thanh Nhan Youth Park*

LAKE DA THIEN (141 E2) *(𝖗 G11)*
Surrounded by hills some 5 km/3.1 mi north of Da Lat is the "Valley of Love". It might initially sound romantic, but it is

in fact an amusement park with countless souvenir shops. Attractions include pony rides, canoes and pedalos. *Daily 8.30am–5pm | admission approx. 26,000 dong*

ON THE ROAD
Do remember to come equipped with plenty of sunscreen and suitable clothing, including some form of sun hat. The sun block must be of a factor high enough to provide protection from the fierce, tropical sun. Parents of very young children should pack pacifiers, bottles, baby food jars and a couple of terry cloth reusable nappies. A baby carrier is certainly useful for overland travel, but on the other hand you should keep luggage volumes to a minimum, particularly if travelling on cramped tourist buses. Everyone, especially children, should drink lots of fluids, but on no account tap water. For reasons of hygiene, only eat ice-cream in a luxury hotel, but it's safer not to buy it at all. It's nearly always possible to rustle up the usual children's staples, such as French fries, ketchup and coke.

TOYS
If your child loses his or her beloved teddy bear, you might be lucky and find an

The family unit is valued highly in Vietnam – so younger travellers are always welcome

identical one to replace it. Or how about a Superman or a panda outfit? You can buy toys in Saigon at *Wooden Toys* (U D3) *(🌣 d3) (Diamond Plaza Shopping Center | 37 Le Duan)*, also (U B2) *(🌣 b2) (142a Ly Chinh Thang)*, and *Kids World* (U E3) *(🌣 e3) (at the Vincom Center | 72 Le Thanh Ton)*. In Hanoi, try *Kids like us* (142 B4) *(🌣 0) (39 Nguyen Thai Hoc | opposite Brothers Café)*. Hanoi's "Toy Road" is called *Luong Van Can* (143 D3) *(🌣 0)*.

WATER PARKS
The numerous water parks, e.g. the amusement and safari park *Vinpearl (phuquoc.vinpearlland.com)* on Phu Quoc, offer many swimming pools, tube slides, water cannons and surfing. The *Dam Sen Water Park* (140 C3) *(🌣 E–F12) (Mon, Wed–Sat 9am–6pm, Sun 8.30am–6pm | avoid weekends | admission approx. 130,000 dong, children 91,000 dong | 3 Hoa Binh | www.damsenwaterpark.com. vn)* in Saigon is an amusement park with rowing boats, giant water slide, *Space Spiral* and a children's railway, likewise in Nha Trang. There is usually a quieter zone for foreigners, but don't expect western standards.

WATER PUPPET THEATRE
The gongs and drums herald in an exciting and funny show in which dragons spew fire and you can hear the rice grow. The puppets, sometimes over 50 cm (20 inches) tall perform on a stage made of water! Very good performances are put on, for example, in Hanoi at the *Thang Long Water Puppet Theatre* (see p. 47) and in Saigon at the *Rong Vang Golden Dragon Water Puppet Theatre* (see p. 98).

ZOOS
You will find zoos and animal parks in many Vietnamese cities and they make popular days out for families. However, it has to be said that the animals are often kept in miserable conditions. And watch out for rusty nails on slides and swings in the parks' playgrounds!

FESTIVALS & EVENTS

Most traditional festivals follow the Chinese lunar calendar. As the lunar month is only 29 or 30 days and the lunar year has 354 or 355 days, every three years between the third and fourth lunar month an extra month is added.

TET NGUYEN DAN

The Chinese and Vietnamese New Year is the most important family event. Celebrations can go on for a week. Flights get booked up very quickly. *(1st day of the 1st month; usually end of Jan/Feb, next dates. 25 Jan 2020, 12 Feb 2021)*

THANH MINH

The Vietnamese people decorate the graves of their relatives with flowers, candles and paper money. *(5th day of the 3rd month; usually in April)*

PHAT DAN

Buddha's birthday is celebrated with processions to the Buddhist pagodas. *(8th day of the 4th month; usually in May)*

TET DOAN NGO

The midsummer festival begins with the symbolic burning of paper sculptures – to drive away the bad spirits from people who are afflicted with a disease. The risk of epidemics is said to be at its greatest at the height of summer. *(5th day of the 5th month; usually end of May/June)*

TRUNG NGUYEN

In the hope that the wandering souls of the long-forgotten dead have no negative impact on an individual's fate, for this holiday offerings in the form of gifts and food are made to altars at home and in temples. *(15th day of the 7th month; usually Aug/Sept)*

TRUNG THU ★

Kind of an extended Valentine's Day: the mid-autumn festival, also known as the children's moon festival, is celebrated with lantern processions at night under a full moon. Special, moon-shaped sticky rice cakes are eaten. This is also the time to celebrate engagements and weddings. *(15th day of the 8th month; usually Sept/Oct)*

Many of Vietnam's celebrations follow the lunar calendar: the ancestors and the spirits have to be honoured – and the governing party

SPRING AND AUTUMN

If you travel through the country in spring or autumn, everywhere, but mainly in the villages, you will see colourful flags – they herald the ★ *Le Hoi festivals*. Le Hoi day is considered the most important event in every village's annual cycle. It is held to honour the village's guardian spirit. After a procession the villagers present a sacrificial offering to the spirit. After that, a lavish banquet is held or plays and concerts performed.

One spectacular celebration is *Le Hoi Choi Trau (8/9th day of the 8th month; usually Sept)*, the village festival in Do Son (25 km/15.5 mi south-east of Hai Phong). After a prelude of music and dancing, two water buffaloes are pitted against each other until one gives up. The owner of the winning buffalo receives a cash prize and then the animal is sacrificed to the harvest god.

APRIL/MAY

To mark the *Huong Tich festival (15th day of the 3rd month; usually April)* grand pilgrimages to the temples of Huong Tich Son take place.

PUBLIC HOLIDAYS

1 Jan	*Tet Duong Lich* (Christian New Year)
3 Feb	Founding of the Vietnamese Communist Party (1930)
30 April	Liberation Day (fall of Saigon to North Vietnamese forces in 1975)
1 May	Labour Day
2 Sept	National day (Declaration of Independence, 1945)

LINKS, BLOGS, APPS & MORE

LINKS & BLOGS

www.thingsasian.com/vietnam One of the best and most colourful sites, covering all aspects of life and travelling in Vietnam. From Adoption to Women & Travel, with travelogues, photos, etc

www.360cities.net/areas/vietnam The 360-degree panoramic photos give an all-round view of top sights. Check out the rotating views of the Mekong Delta, Phong Nha Cave, Ha Long Bay, Hoi An by night, even Saigon General Post Office

vietnamesegod.blogspot.com "Funny guy" from Nha Trang tells about his experiences in Vietnam: weddings, temple visits, recipes, tips – a glimpse of the young and modern side of Vietnam from the inside

www.insideasiatours.com/inside vietnam/blog Interesting and up-to-date information about everything tourists need to know in Vietnam, but also in Laos and Cambodia

www.eatingsaigon.com Subtitled "Saigon Street Food Adventures", this great site describes the best street food stalls of the city according to categories such as "Seafood", "Desserts" or "Gay Saigon". Plus: You can book a dinner with a local family

www.theravenouscouple.com Hong and Kim, a couple living in Los Angeles, share their delicious Vietamese recipes, accompanied by mouth-watering pictures and instructive videos

hello-saigon.com Extensive blog by a Saigon resident who's been living there for six years

blog.madsmonsen.com A photo studio based in saigon shares

Regardless of whether you are still researching your trip or already in Vietnam: these addresses will provide you with more information, videos and networks to make your holiday even more enjoyable

some great photography (from New Year's fireworks to Vietnamese children) which get you into the right mood

twitter.com/HanoiGrapevine Twitter is quite popular in Vietnam: check out these posts about the young art and culture scene in the country

hanoiebuddies.com.vn This volunteers' association offers free tours of Hanoi. The students show sides of the city seldom seen by tourists and other visitors in English-speaking tours, offering an authentic glimpse into the culture of Vietnam

VIDEOS & MUSIC

www.huongthanh.com Contemporary music by popular singer Huong Thanh. Melancholic sounds in traditional style, perfect for a boat trip through a misty Ha Long Bay

www.youtube.com/watch?v=XgWOo-Ui94k A ten-minute documentary about the Vietnam War, so you'll know all about the basic facts

www.youtube.com/watch?v=-JNWucQJGVI Just so you know what could await you on the streets of Saigon...

www.facebook.com/suboimusic Suboi already performed rap in front of Barack Obama who set the rhythm. The rapper queen from Saigon writes and sings ambivalent and critical lyrics – between the lines.

APPS

Vietnamese Phrasebook Offers essential phrases for free, also has quizzes and study flip cards. simplylearnlanguages.com/vietnamese

Vietnamese recipes Free app with recipes to recreate at home

TRAVEL TIPS

ARRIVAL

✈ Vietnam Airlines fly non-stop every day from London to Saigon and Hanoi (approx. £600). A number of airlines, including Vietnam Airlines, Qatar Airways and American Airlines, fly from New York, Los Angeles and other cities (from US$800). When booking onward flights within Vietnam or to neighbouring countries, the Vietnamese national carrier often grants a discount of 50 percent. www.vietnamairlines.com

BANKS, MONEY & CURRENCY

Opening times for Vietnamese banks are normally as follows: Mon–Fri 7.30am–11.30am and 1.30pm–3.30pm or 4pm. However, these times can often vary.
The Vietnamese Dong (VND) is the local currency. Always check the digits when handling the notes. They range in value from 500 to 500,000 VND. For everyday transactions use the 10,000, 50,000, 100,000 notes and in more expensive restaurants the 500,000 note. Even if prices are given in US dollars, always pay in dong. There are ATM machines in all towns and you can use your Visa and MasterCard cards to draw Vietnamese dong from them, but you should expect to pay a small fee. You can change dollars without any problem (make sure you have your passport with you). Large hotels, tourist restaurants, travel agencies and airline offices accept credit cards (up to 4 percent handling fee). For safety's sake, it's a good idea to keep a few US dollars on you, particularly if you're planning to move on to Cambodia or are likely to arrive at Hanoi airport late at night. The official bank exchange rate is often less favourable (by approx. 2,500 VND) at the airport; it is better in hotels and in large towns. It is recommended to use the licensed, privately-run change bureaux (usually open from 7am–10pm, e.g. in Dong Khoi street or in Saigon's General Post Office) or in larger jewellery shops. As the theft of smaller sums of money from rooms, luggage, even room safes, is not uncommon, if possible leave your money in the safe at reception and ask for a receipt.

RESPONSIBLE TRAVEL

It doesn't take a lot to be environmentally friendly whilst travelling. Don't just think about your carbon footprint whilst flying to and from your holiday destination but also about how you can protect nature and culture abroad. As a tourist it is especially important to respect nature, look out for local products, cycle instead of driving, save water and much more. If you would like to find out more about eco-tourism please visit: www.ecotourism.org

CLIMATE, WHEN TO GO

If you go to the south, then the best time is between December and March, when the temperatures are bearable and there is little rainfall. In April/May, it can be oppressively sultry ahead of the rainy season (from June to December). The months of June to October bring heavy

From arrival to weather

Your holiday from start to finish: the most important addresses and information for your Vietnam trip

storms and occasionally floods to central Vietnam and the Mekong Delta region. The further north you go, the greater the differences between summer and winter. Whereas sub-tropical summers from April onwards can be hot and humid, from December to February the temperatures on the central/north coast can fall well below 20 °C/68 °F. In addition, long periods of drizzle can spoil the enjoyment of travel.

CONSULATES & EMBASSIES

UK EMBASSY HANOI
Central Building, 4th floor | 31 Hai Ba Trung | Hanoi | tel. 04 39 36 05 00 | http://ukinvietnam.fco.gov.uk/en/

UK CONSULATE HO CHI MINH CITY
25 Le Duan Street | District 1 | Ho Chi Minh City| tel. 028 38 25 13 80

US EMBASSY HANOI
7 Lang Ha Street | tel. 024 38 50 50 00 | Hanoi | vn.usembassy.gov

US CONSULATE HO CHI MINH CITY
4 Le Duan Blvd. Dist. 1 | Ho Chi Minh City | tel. 028 35 20 42 00 | hochiminh.uscon sulate.gov

CUSTOMS

1.5 l of high-percentage alcohol or 2 l wine and 200 cigarettes or 100 cigars or 500 g/1.1 lbs tobacco may be imported into Vietnam duty-free. If you wish to export antiques, you will need to obtain an export certificate. The following quantities may be imported into EU (per person aged 18 or above): 200 cigarettes, 50 cigars or 500 g/1.1 lbs tobac-

co, 1 l alcohol above and 2 l alcohol up to 22 vol.% and 4 l of wine, other goods such as tea, perfume and gifts up to a value of £380/US$500.

CURRENCY CONVERTER

£	VND	VND	£
1	30,450	10,000	0.33
2	60,900	20,000	0.66
3	91,350	30,000	0.99
4	121,800	40,000	1.32
5	152,250	50,000	1.65
6	182,700	60,000	1.98
7	213,150	70,000	2.31
8	243,600	80,000	2.64
9	274,050	90,000	2.97

US$	VND	VND	US$
1	23,200	10,000	0.43
2	46,400	20,000	0.86
3	69,600	30,000	1.29
4	92,800	40,000	1.72
5	116,000	50,000	2.15
6	139,200	60,000	2.58
7	185,600	70,000	3.01
8	178,428	80,000	3.44
9	208,800	90,000	3.87

For current exchange rates see www.xe.com

ELECTRICITY

Mains voltage is usually 220V. Remember to pack a universal adapter.

HEALTH

No vaccinations are required, unless you have arrived from a yellow-fever zone. However, protection against polio, tetanus, diphtheria, hepatitis A/B and typhus is recommended. A stand-by medication is advisable in malaria regions. To avoid diarrhoea, do not drink tap water or even use it to clean your teeth. Do not eat unpeeled fruit or salad, unless you are dining in an international hotel. The same advice applies to ice-cream. Because of the risk of cholera in north Vietnam (mainly Hanoi and

a hospital specialising in tropical medicine. A health insurance policy is essential. Make sure cover includes medical evacuation costs.

IMMIGRATION/VISAS

Tourist visas, issued only by Vietnamese embassies, are valid for up to four weeks and permit a single entry. The cost of a 15-day visa £50/US$75, for 30 days £58/US$85. To apply for a visa in the UK or the US, check the website of the relevant Vietnamese embassy (see below), where you can download an application form. The normal processing period for a tourist visa is 5 days, but an express service is possible for an extra charge. You must forward your passport, a passport photo and the payment by cheque. Alternatively, you can apply in person. When you arrive in Vietnam, you must fill in an entry form and customs declaration, a duplicate of which must be submitted when you leave.

EMBASSIES OF THE SOCIALIST REPUBLIC OF VIETNAM

– 12 Victoria Road | London W8 5RD | tel. 020 7937 1912 | www.vietnamembassy. org.uk
– 1233 20th Street | NW Suite 400 | Washington, DC 20036 | tel. 0202 8 61 07 37 | vietnamembassy-usa.org

---

BUDGETING

Coffee	£0.45/US$0.60 *for one cup in a Vietnamese café*
Noodle soup	£0.90–1.75/US$1.15–2.30 *in a Vietnamese restaurant*
Taxi ride	£0.50/US$0.65 *per kilometre*
Beer	from £0.18/US$0.25 *for a draught beer in a Vietnamese bar*
Dress	from £26/US$35 *for an ao dai dress*
Massage	£5.30–7/US$7–9.30 *on the beach*

Ninh Binh), it is probably better to avoid it altogether. Vaccination against cholera is no longer a requirement for entry into any country, but a well-tolerated oral vaccine against cholera is available. Dengue fever has been reported in the south of Vietnam, mainly in the Mekong Delta region, but also in Saigon. The virus is transmitted by a mosquito, which is active during the daytime. The best form of prevention is to wear bright, long-sleeved clothing and use a mosquito repellent. There is no vaccine. For up-to-date information, contact your doctor's surgery or consult the website of

INFORMATION

ICS TRAVEL GROUP
870 Market Street, Suite 923 | San Francisco, CA 94102 | USA | tel. 0415 434 4015 | icstravelgroup.com

VIETNAM NATIONAL ADMINISTRATION OF TOURISM
80 Quan Su | Hanoi | tel. 024 39 42 37 60 | www.vietnam-tourism.com

SAIGON TOURIST

23 Le Loi | 1st district | tel. 028 38 29 22 91 | hotline (nationwide) tel. 19 00 18 08 | www.saigon-tourist.com

FOCUS ASIA

138a Nguyen Dinh Chieu | Saigon | tel. 028 38 22 82 20 | www.focus.asia

If there is no tourist office where you are staying, your hotel will provide you with information.

INTERNET & WIFI

Internet access is available for free almost everywhere (except for some luxury hotels): hotels and cafés, airports and even some bus stations and (overnight) buses (*Mai Linh* and *Phuong Trang/Futa*, very slow and it pays to have a pre-paid card). There are Internet cafés all over the country where you can Skype, even in isolated mountain regions. The government blocks social networks every now and then, but you can often circumvent this problem by using a proxy server (look into one ahead of time).

NEWSPAPERS

There are two English-language newspapers: "Saigon Times Weekly" and "Vietnam News" *(www.vietnamnews.com.vn)*. Most large hotels, international bookshops and street vendors in town centres sell the main foreign press titles. Tourists often find "Time Out Vietnam" and "The Guide" useful.

OPENING HOURS & ADMISSION CHARGES

Do not expect opening times to be punctually adhered to. Many museums are closed on Mon or at least from 11.30am to 1.30pm. Unless otherwise stated, admission is free.

PHONE & MOBILE PHONE

The country code for the UK is 0044, USA 001 and Vietnam 0084. Then dial the local area code without the zero.

Calling abroad from your hotel can cost less than £0.45/US$0.60 per minute. It is often cheaper to use an IDD phone card obtainable from post offices and some telephone kiosks (up to approx. £0.18/US$0.23 per minute). Cheapest of all are the internet cafés (e.g. with Skype or Yahoo! Voice it's free, but often with poor connections. Turning off the webcam can help to improve sound quality). Free of charge is phoning via internet (e.g. Whatsapp).

The mobile phone providers are *Viettel* and the more expensive *Vinaphone* and *Mobiphone*. Using a foreign SIM card in Vietnam can be expensive. If you are using a British or American provider, extra hidden charges are added by the Vietnamese companies to incoming calls, in some cases up to £0.80/1.20US$ per minute. For information on the roaming agreement: *www.gsmworld.com*. Save money on calls home with a prepaid 1718 card; the low-cost code 1718 (+0044) makes calls to the UK cheap. You can also get family members or friends to call you back. From the UK and USA to Vietnam: either via Skype or with scratch cards from in Asian food shops. With the latter, you can speak for approx. 250 minutes for £4.40/US$5.80, e.g. *www.nobelphonecard.com* or *www.nobelphonecard.uk*.

Vietnamese SIM cards/pre-paid cards are adapted by SIM-card street traders or small shops everywhere, then the phone call back home is relatively reasonable, for example, with *Happy Tourist* from Mobiphone for approx. £9/US$11.50; the price varies according to the data volume up to 6 GB and account (approx. £0.15/US$0.25) per minute and text messages (approx. £0.08/US$0.13) to Europe and

North America), however you will need an unlock code and you will be allocated a new telephone number (or buy a new mobile phone for £8–12/US$13–17 in Vietnam). As there are many expensive telephone numbers (e.g. the easy to remember 4 00 40 04 00), when you buy, make sure you ask for a "cheap" number.

POST

Airmail deliveries to Europe and the USA can take up to three weeks (a stamp for a postcard is approx. £0.35/US$0.50). Only post letters or cards in post offices in the larger towns or in quality hotels. If you want to send a parcel, it can be expensive and unreliable. Better to use a courier service, such as DHL (counter in Saigon General Post Office).

TAXI & RICKSHAW

In Hanoi and in Saigon, many taxis have taximeters (approx. £0.48/US$0.64 per km). Unfortunately, some taxi drivers in Hanoi and Saigon do use various tricks to swindle their passengers. If the figure on the taximeter appears to be rising rapidly and the driver keeps beeping his horn, ask him to stop, pay the stated sum and get out quickly. If you want a taxi from your hotel, order an official taxi or only use official, reputable companies. In Saigon *Vinasun (tel. 028 38 27 27 27)* and *Vinataxi (tel. 028 38 11 11 11)* are reliable and *May Linh (nationwide tel. 10 55)* throughout Vietnam. Also in Hanoi and Vietnam: *www.uber.com*. Cyclos, i.e. cycle-hauled rickshaws, are typical; it is normal to negotiate a price in advance (approx. 52,000–

WEATHER IN SAIGON

	Jan	Feb	March	April	May	June	July	Aug	Sept	Oct	Nov	Dec
Daytime temperatures in °C/°F	32/90	33/91	34/93	35/95	33/91	32/90	31/88	31/88	31/88	31/88	31/88	31/88
Nighttime temperatures in °C/°F	21/70	22/72	23/73	24/75	24/75	24/75	24/75	24/75	23/73	23/73	23/73	22/72
Sunshine hours/day	6	8	7	7	5	5	5	5	5	5	5	6
Precipitation days/month	2	1	2	4	16	21	23	21	21	20	11	7
Water temperature in °C/°F	24/75	25/77	25/77	28/82	28/82	28/82	28/82	28/82	28/82	27/81	27/81	25/77

104,000 dong per hour; in Saigon/1st district and Hanoi/Old Quarter prices can get over the top around 208,000 dong, it depends on your negociation skills). Moped taxis are also popular (always wear a helmet). In many cities, such as Can Tho, there are motorised cyclo taxis, i.e. a moped in front of a two-seater carriage (approx. 13,000 dong per kilometre). As it is difficult for tourists to figure out how the rather sparse public bus service operates (only in Saigon and Hanoi) and Saigon's underground is not due to be completed until 2020, the taxi in all its different manifestations will for some time yet continue to be the main way of getting around.

TIME

Vietnam time is seven hours ahead of Greenwich Mean Time, during the summer only six hours ahead; it is 15 hours ahead of Standard Pacific Time and 12 hours ahead of Eastern Standard Time.

TIPPING

Feel free to tip good service, but in the better-class restaurants and hotels, it is often retained as a service charge. Tips are not expected at the food stalls. In hotels, you can tip about 20,000–30,000 dong per day. On group trips, a tip will usually be collected at the end for the driver and the tour guide, approx. 150,000 dong per person per day for both together.

TRAVEL & TOURS IN VIETNAM

Vietnam Airlines operate daily flights linking all the major cities. A Saigon to Hanoi return ticket (2-hour flight) costs from £120/US$160, much less with the low-cost airlines *Viet Jet Air (www.vietjetair. com)* and *Jetstar Pacific Vietnam (www.jetstar.com)*. You must book well in advance during the Tet Festival. Trains also run regularly between Hanoi and Saigon. A journey on the *Reunification Express* between north and south is a good way to see the country (it runs five times a day there and back), the journey takes 32–38 hours. Book a 1st class *Soft Sleeper* ticket and do so well in advance.

Travelling by public overland bus is not advisable, as there have been many serious accidents. If you want to travel on a tourist bus, ask in the traveller cafés about *Open Tours*. The buses, with reclining seats, are new (Hanoi to Hue costs approx. £13/US$17). *Mai Linh Express Bus (tel. 028 39 39 39 39 | www.mailinghexpress.vn)* and *Hoang Long (tel. 0225 3 92 09 20 | hoanglongasia.com)* are reliable bus companies. Online tickets for plane/train/bus, also via credit card, are available e.g. from *www. baolau.vn*, *www.12go.asia/en* and *dsvn.vn*. A hire car with driver is the time-honoured way to tour the country. Ask for details in your hotel or better still at a travel agency. Costs, including driver and petrol, start at approx. £40/US$52 per day, plus a fee for a guide (£26/US$35), if you wish. Tourists need an international driving permit to drive a car; riding a moped with more than 50 cc dispalcement is officially not permitted (and dangerous). International car rental companies: *Avis (www.avis.com.vn), VN Rent a Car (www. vnrentacar.com)* ● Mekong Delta tours: *Mekong Eyes Cruise (Can Tho | www. mekongeyes.com)* organise boat tours on a converted rice barge with 30 nice double rooms. Another good tour operator is *Sinh Balo Adventure Travel (283/ 20 Pham Ngu Lao | Saigon | tel. 028 38 37 67 66 | www.sinhbalo.com | two days for two persons approx. £123/US$162 per person)*. If you want luxury travel, then investigate *Pandaw ships (www.pandaw. com)*, which run between Saigon/My Tho and Angkor in Cambodia.

USEFUL PHRASES
VIETNAMESE

PRONUNCIATION

For ease of pronunciation all Vietnamese words are provided with a simple pronunciation guide [in square brackets]. The following characters (left column) are special characters and are pronounced as follows (right column):

c	c as in "cat" mixed with g as in "go"	ph	ph as in "phone"	Tones:	
		tr	ch as in "chip"	a	flat
-ch	ck as in "lick"	x	s as in "hiss"	á	high rising like "day"
đ/Đ	d as in "dog"	â	u as in "hut"		
d/gi-	z as in "zip"	e	eah as in "yeah"	ã	creaky
kh-	ch as in Scottish "loch"	ê	ay as in "lay"	à	falling
		ơ	ur	ạ	falling, then rising
ch-	ch as in "chip"	ú	oo		
nh-	ny			ạ	a low "a-ah"

IN BRIEF

Yes (according to region)	có [goh]; ừ [ur]; dạ [dya]
No/Maybe	không [kong]/có lẽ [goh lay]
Please/	Xin [seen], Làm ơ n [lahm oin]
Thank you	Cám ởn [gam un]
Excuse me, please!	Tôi xin lỗi! [toy seen loy]
Pardon?	Xin nhắc lại? [seen nyac lai]
I would like to...	Tôi muôñ... [toy mu-en]
How much is...?	Gía bao nhiêu? [zhah bao nyu]
I (don't) like that	Tôi rât/không thích [toy rut/kong thik]
good/bad	tốt [toht]/xâú [sao]
too much/much/little	thât nhiêu [tut nyu]/nhiêù [nyu]/ít [eet]
all/nothing	tâc cả [tuk gah]/không [kong]
Help!	Xin giúp tôi! [seen zyub toy]
ambulance	Xe cứu thương [say kyu tur-ong]
Prohibition/forbidden	câm [gam]
danger/dangerous	nguy hiêm [nyee hem]
May I take your picture?	Tôi đúôc phep chup anh? [toy dur feb dyub an]

GREETINGS, FAREWELL

Good morning!/afternoon/ Good evening!/night!/Hello!	Xin chào! [seen chao]

BẠN NÓI ĐƯỢC TIẾNG VIỆT KHÔNG?

"Do you speak Vietnamese?" This guide will help you to say the basic words and phrases in Vietnamese

Goodbye!/See you	Chào tạm biệt! [chao tam bee-et]
My name is...	Tên tôi là... [tu-en toyla]
What's your name?	Anh/Chi tên gí? [an/chee tu-en zee] (masc/fem)

DATE & TIME

Monday/Tuesday	thứ hai [too hai]/thứ ba [too bah]
Wednesday/Thursday	thứ tư [too du]/thứ năm [too nam]
Friday/Saturday	thứ sáu [too sao]/thứ bãy [too bai]
Sunday	chũ nhât [choo nyut]
holiday/	ngáy nghí [nyai nyee]/
working day	ngáy lam viêc [nyai lahm vee-ek]
today/tomorrow/	hôm này [hom nai]/ngáy may [nyai mai]/
yesterday	hôm qua [hom kwah]
hour/minute	giờ [zur]/phút [phoot]
day/night/week	ngáy [nyai]/đem [daym]/tuân [twun]
What time is it?	Mây giờ rôî? [mai zur roy]
It's three o'clock	Bây giờ là ba giờ [bai-ee zur la bah zur]
It's half past three	Bây giờ la ba mùoi [bai-ee zur la bah moy]

TRAVEL

open/closed	mở [mur]/đóng [dong]
entrance/exit	lôí vào [loy vao]/lôí ra [loy rah]
departure/departure (plane)	khợi hánh [koy hahn]
toilets (ladies/gentlemen)	nhà vê sinh (nữ/nam) [nya vay sin (nur/nahm)]
(no) drinking water	(không) nước uông [(kong) nyok wong]
Where is...?/Where are...?	ở đâu vây...? [ur duh vay]/ở đâu vây...? [ur duh veh]
left/right	trái [chai]/phải [phai]
straight ahead/back	thăng tới [tang toy]/lui lại [lui lai]
close/far	gân [guhn]/xa [sah]
street map/map	bán đồ [ban doh]
bus/tram/taxi	bus [boos]/táu điên [tao dee-en]/tă'c-xi [taksee]
bus stop	trạm xe bus [chahm say boos]
parking lot	nổi đổ xe [noy doh say]
train station/harbour	nhà ga [nya gah]/bên cảng [ben cang]
airport	sận bay [shun bai]
single/return	đơn giãn [don zyan]/tỏi vá lúi [toy vah lui]
train / track/platform	táu [tao]/đuóng rây [dur-ong ray]
I would like to rent...	Tôi muồn thuê... [toy mu-en too-ay]
a car/a bicycle	ô-tô [otoh]/xe đạp [say dap]
petrol/gas station	trạm xăng đâù [chahm sang dao]

FOOD & DRINK

Could you please book a table for tonight for four?	ông/bà làm ơn cho chúng tôi một bàn bốn người tối nay [ong/bah lahm oin, cho choong toy moh' ban bohn nyu-ay toy nai]
on the terrace	hanh lang [han lang]
by the window	cửa sổ [koo-a soh]
The menu, please	Làm ơn cho tôi thực đơn [lam oin cho toy took doin]
salt/pepper/sugar	muối [moy]/tiêu [tiu]/đường [dur-ong]
cold/too salty/ not cooked	lanh [lan]/mặn [mang]/ chưa chín [chu-a chin]
with/without ice	có đá [koh dah]/không có đá [kong koh dah]
fizzy/still	có gas [koh gas]/không có gas [kong koh gas]
vegetarian/allergy	người ăn chay [noy an chai]/dị ứng [dyay loong]
May I have the bill, please	Làm o´n tính tiền [lam oin, teen dee-en]

SHOPPING

Where can I find...?	ở đâu có...? [ur dao goh...]
pharmacy/chemist	nhà thuốc tây [nya tuok tai]
shopping centre/market	cửa hàng [ku-a hang]/chợ [chur]
kiosk	tạp hóa [tahp hwa]
100 grammes/ 1 kilo	một trăm gram [moht cham gram]/ một kilo [moht kilo]
expensive/cheap	Đặt [dat] / ré [ray]
more/less	nhiêu [nyu]/ít [eet]

ACCOMMODATION

I have booked a room	Tôi có một phòng đả đặt trước [toy goh moh phong dah dut choo]
Do you have any... left?	ông/bà có còn...? [ong/bah goh con...]
single room	phòng đồn [phong don]
double room	phòng đôi [phong doy]
shower/sit-down bath	Với phòng tăm [voy phong tum]
balcony/terrace	balkon/sân thừong [shun tur-ong]

BANKS, MONEY & CREDIT CARDS

bank/ATM	bank [bank] (ngân hàng) [nan hang]/ nổi lấy tiền tự đông [noy lay dee-en tu dong]
I'd like to change...	Tôi muôn đồi... thành tiền [toy mu-en doy... tan dee-en]
cash/credit card	tiền mặt [dee-en mut]/thẻ tín dụng [tay teen zoong]
change	đồi tiền [doy dee-en]

HEALTH

doctor/dentist/ paediatrician	bắć sĩ [bak shee]/nha sĩ [nya shee]/ bắć sĩ nhi đống [bak shee nyee dong]
hospital	bênh viên [ben vee-en]
fever/pain	sốt [shoht]/đau [dao]
diarrhoea/nausea	tiêu chảy [dee-u chai]/ói mử [oy mur]
inflamed/injured	bị viêm [bee vee-em] / bị thươ'ng [bee tur-ong]
plaster/bandage	Cứu th ươ' ng cá nhân [kyu tur-ong gah nyun]
pain reliever/tablet	thuốc chóng đau [too-ok chong dao]/Thuốc [too-ok]

POST, TELECOMMUNICATIONS & MEDIA

stamp/letter	tem [tem]/thư [too]
postcard	bưu thiếp [boo tee-ep]
Where can I find internet access?	Nổi truy câp internet? [noy chee gup internet]
socket/adapter/ charger	ổ căm điện [oh gahm dee-en]/biến thế [bee-en tay]/ máy nạp điện [mai nap dee-en]
dial/connection/ engaged	quay số [kwai soh]/nối kêt [noy kurt]/ máy đang bân [mai dan bun]
e-mail address/ internet address (URL)/ at sign (@)	địa chỉ điện tín [dee-a chee dee-en teen]/ địa chỉ điện tín [dee-a chee dee-en teen]/ a còng [ah gong]
internet connection/wifi	Internet/sóng [song]
e-mail/file/print	E-Mail/hộp chửa [hob chua]/in ra [een rah]

LEISURE, SPORTS & BEACH

beach/lido	bải tăm [bai tam]/hố bởi [hoh boy]
sunshade/lounger	ô [ouh]/ghế bố [gay boh]
low tide/high tide/ current	thưy triêu [too-ee chee-oo]/bảo lut [bao lood]/ nước chảy [nyok chai]

NUMBERS

0	không [kong]	10	mười [moy]
1	một [moht]	20	hai mười [hai moy]
2	hai [hai]	70	bảy mười [bai moy]
3	ba [bah]	100	một trăm [moht cham]
4	bốn [bohn]	200	hai trăm [hai cham]
	năm [nam]	1,000	một ngàn [moht nyan]
	sáu [sao]	2,000	hai ngàn [hai nyan]
	bảy [bai]	10,000	mười ngàn [moy nyan]
	tám [dahm]	½	một phân hai [moht phan hai]
	chín [cheen]	¼	một phân tư [moht phan dur]

ROAD ATLAS

The green line indicates the Discovery Tour "Vietnam at a glance"
The blue line indicates the other Discovery Tours

All tours are also marked on the pull-out map

Photo: Fishermen near Mui Ne

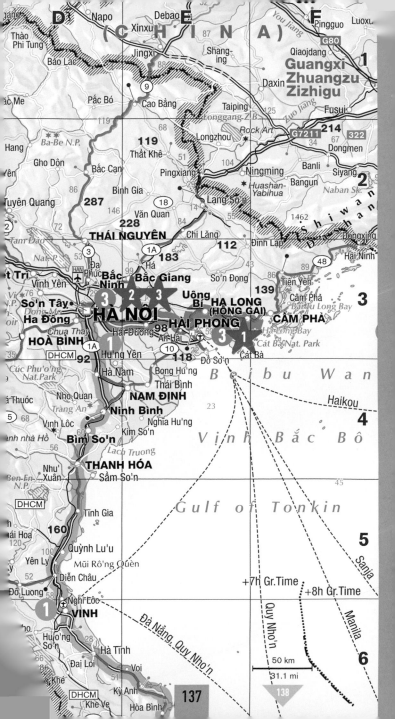

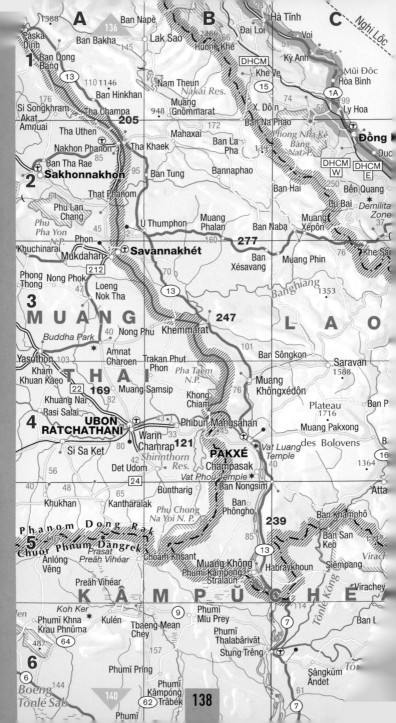

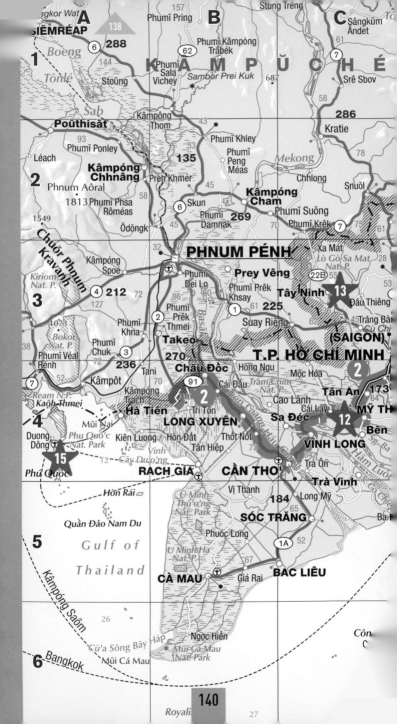

Angkor Wat **A** 138 **B** 157 Stung Treng **C** To
SIEMRÉAP 288 Phumĭ Pring Sângkŭm Ándet
1 Boeng 6 144 62 Phumĭ Kâmpóng Trâbêk 61 **7**
Tônlé Phumĭ Sala Vichey Sâmbor Prei Kuk 687 Srê Sbov
Stoŭng K Â M P U C H É
Sab Kâmpóng Thom 43 58 **286**
Poŭthĭsăt 93 Mekong Kratie 78
Léach Phumĭ Ponley Preh Khmêr 53 Phumĭ Khley Chhlong
2 Kâmpóng Chhnăng Phumĭ Peng Méas Snuŏl
Phnum Aôral 58 **135** Skun Kâmpóng Cham
1813 Phumĭ Phsa Rôméas 6 Phumĭ Suŏng Phumĭ Krêk 75
1549 Ŏdŏngk 45 **269** 70 7 61
Chŭŏr Phnum Kravanh Kâmpóng Spœ Phumĭ Dei Lo 32 **PHNUM PÉNH** Xa Mát 28
Kiriom Nat. P. 4 **212** 72 Phumĭ Prêk Thmei Phumĭ Prêk Khsay 60 **Prey Vêng** Lô Gò Sa Mát Nats.P. 53
3 127 Phumĭ Khna 2 Basăk 61 225 Tây Ninh 22B **13** Đâu Thiêng
1073 Bokor Nat. P. Phumĭ Chuk 3 Takeo Suay Riêng Tràng Bàng Củ Chi
38 Phumĭ Véal Rénh 72 **236** **270** Châu Đôc Hồng Ngự **T.P. HỒ CHÍ MINH** (SAIGON)
Ream N.P. 52 7 Tani Kâmpôt Kâmpóng Trach 70 91 716 Cái Đâu Mộc Hóa Tân An 173
Kaôh-Thmei Hà Tiên Tri Tôn Trâm Chim Nat. P. Cao Lãnh Cái Lây **MỸ TH**
4 Mũi Nai **LONG XUYÊN** Sa Đéc **12** Bên
Dương Đông Phu Quốc Nat. Park Kiên Lương Hòn Đât Tân Hiệp Thôt Nôt 73 **VĨNH LONG** Hàm Luô
15 Vĩnh Cây Dương T2 **RẠCH GIÁ** **CÂN THƠ** Trà Ôn Bê
Phú Quốc Hòn Rái Vị Thanh Long Mỹ Trà Vinh
Quần Đảo Nam Du U Minh Thượng Nat. Park **184**
5 Gulf Phước Long **SÓC TRĂNG** Ba
Kâmpóng Saôm of U Minh Hạ Nat. P. 1A 52
Thailand 65
Cù'a Sông Bây Háp 26 **CÀ MAU** Giá Rai 67 **BẠC LIÊU**
6 Bangkok Mũi Cá Mau Ngọc Hiển Mũi Cá Mau Nat. Park Côn C
140
Royali 27

Lomphat
Srepok
Phumĭ Klâng
Khval
Ban Đôn
Senmonorom
Rang
Phumĭ Leu
Tanh Hóa
Long
Đông Phú
Thánh
Trị An Lake
hủ Hung
Ù DẦU MỘT
BIÊN HÒA
Long Thành
Bình Giã
Phú Mỹ
ước
Ô Cộng
ồng
Can Gio
Mangrove Biosph. Res.
Soi Rạp
ng Hậu
a Sông Cửu Long
ouths of the Mekong)

D **E** **F**

Đèo Tu Na **119**
Cheo Reo **1318** La Hai Sông Cầu
Chí Thanh
Krông Pa **139**
29 **Tuy Hòa**
Ea Sup
Ea H'leo
DHCM
Krong Buk
B.E. Klô'p
179 **74**
Tãy So'n
62 **90**
147
M' Drac **1731** 28 Vành Ninh
108 **BUÔN MA THUỘT** Dục Mỹo Ninh Hòa 95
Chư Đang Sin Dục Mỹo
1673 2405 Chu Yang Sin 36 **NHA TRANG**
Đăk Mil 47 Lặc Lạc Lake N.P. Diên Phước 50
Đắc Song 27 Bidoup Núi Bà So'n Hiệp Hòn Tre **2**
5 N.P. 1A **136**
Bù Gia Mập 1580 127 Lạc Duong **ĐÀ LẠT** So'n
Nat. P. Dak Nông To' Lan Prenn Falls 69 **CAM RANH**
253 63 Đức Trong 68 Ninh
Bù Đang 1/465 Đèo 32 Đo'n 137 So'n 50 Vĩnh Hy
Đức Liễu Ông Cọ Du'o'ng Núi Chúa
Nam Cát Di Linh 48 Văn Lần **4** Nat. Park
Tien N.P. 1864 PHAN RANG-
Bảo Lộc 20 54 THÁP CHÀM
Ma M'rê 51 122
204 Ma Đa Gui 1545 Bắc Bình Tùy Phong 200 **3**
Tân Phú Tánh Linh Sông Lũy 55 Mũi La Gan
4 Xuân Lộc Ham Thuận **14** 26 Mũi Né
1 Tân Minh Nam **288** PHAN THIẾT
11 Tan Minh 57
51 La Gi Mũi Kê Gà
Long Điền Vĩnh Phạm Thiêv
Mũi Kỳ Vận 85 Phù Qúy
Long Hải (Cù Lao Thu)
VŨNG TÀU

4
7
Yusun Shoal

S O U T H

C H I N A

S E A **5**

50 km
31.1 mi **6**
860

141

D   E   F

1

Biên
Long
Cầu

Huyện Gia Lâm
Ái Mô

Bus Station

Nguyễn Văn Cừ

2

Trần Khoai
ng Xuan ết
oi Boutique el?)
Nhất
Phúc

Chiêu
Nguyễn Siêu
Chua Bach Ma
Röhrenhaus

Duong Nguyen
Tân

Cầu Chương Dương

Phú Viên

Hàng
Bưởm
Ma Mây

H. Đạo

Hàng

Gia Ngư'
Trần Nguyên Huấn

Bạch

Sông Hồng

3

Cầu
Gỗ
Đinh
H. Thùng

Den Ngoc Son

Port

Water Puppetry Theatre

Quận Hoàn Kiếm

Hồ Hoàn Kiếm

Trần Nguyên Hân
Culture House

Tông
Quang

4

chua a Da

Tô.

Thi

Hương
Bà
Bái
Hàng Khay
Tràng

Park I. Gandhi
Bank

National Bank

Đạn
Khải

General Post Office

Hotel Sofitel Metropole

Tiên
Lê

Museum of Revolution

Le Bon Café
Historical Museum

Trần

Tru'ng
Opera

Pham

Museum of Women
Đường

Chu'o'ng Kiệt

Geological Museum

Ngu Lao

Vietnam Tourism

Thanh

Police
Hưng

Tôn

5

Đạo
Phan

Đặng

Restaurant AuLac House

Trần

Hàng

Khánh

st ice

Hàng
Ngô

Hang

Thanh

Hospital

Youth Theatre

Lô

Huu Nghi Hospital

Theatre

Mã

Chuoi

Trừ

Tông

Dư

Ha Noi

6

inh
Hoà
Pharmacy
Service

Nguyễn
Công
Đức

500 m
547 yd

Huế

Quận Hai Bà Trưng
Den Hai Ba Trung

143

INDEX

This index lists all places and destinations mentioned in the guide. Page numbers in bold type refer to the main entry.

CREDITS

WRITE TO US

e-mail: info@marcopologuides.co.uk
Did you have a great holiday?
Is there something on your mind?
Whatever it is, let us know!
Whether you want to praise, alert us
to errors or give us a personal tip –
MARCO POLO would be pleased to
hear from you.
We do everything we can to provide the
very latest information for your trip.

Nevertheless, despite all of our authors'
thorough research, errors can creep in.
MARCO POLO does not accept any
liability for this. Please contact us by
e-mail or post.
MARCO POLO Travel Publishing Ltd
Pinewood, Chineham Business Park
Crockford Lane, Chineham
Basingstoke, Hampshire RG24 8AL
United Kingdom

PICTURE CREDITS
Cover photograph: Halong Bay (Look: Per-Andre Hoffmann)
Photos: DuMont Bildarchiv: Krause (34, 75, 81, 119, 120/121, 123); Getty Images/Robert Harding World Imagery: Francis (113); huber-images: T. Draper (41), P. Giocoso (4 bottom), Gräfenhain (4 top, 37, 82, 92), R. Taylor (5); huber-images/Picture Finders (25); F. Ihlow (29, 42); Laif: F. Heuer (22), M. Sasse (2, 89, 91, 97), I. Sciacca (19 bottom); Laif/Aurora: B. Wald (7); Look: Per-Andre Hoffmann (1); mauritius images: Kugler (61); mauritius images/age (38); mauritius images/Alamy (3, 6, 12/13, 58, 65, 67, 70, 110); mauritius images/imagebroker: J. Beck (69), B. Bieder (102/103), G. Zwerger-Schoner (50); mauritius images/robertharding (54/55); picture alliance: M. Drobeck (18 bottom), C. Kaster (19 top), Kham (18 centre), W. Perugini (18 top); D. Renckhoff (118); T. Stankiewicz (8, 63); M. Weigt (flap left, 9, 10, 11, 14/15, 17, 20/21, 26/27, 28 left, 28 right, 30, 30/31, 31, 32/33, 44, 46, 49, 53, 56, 60, 66, 72, 76/77, 78, 83, 85, 86, 94, 99, 108, 114/115, 116/117, 118/119, 120, 121, 122 top, 122 bottom, 134/135); White Star: Schiefer (flap right, 101)

3rd edition – fully revised and updated 2020
Worldwide Distribution: Marco Polo Travel Publishing Ltd, Pinewood, Chineham Business Park, Crockford Lane, Basingstoke, Hampshire RG24 8AL, United Kingdom. Email: sales@marcopolouk.com
© MAIRDUMONT GmbH & Co. KG , Ostfildern
Chief editor: Stefanie Penck
Author: Martina Miethig; editor: Corinna Walkenhorst
Cartography road atlas: © MAIRDUMONT, Ostfildern; cartography pull-out map: © MAIRDUMONT, Ostfildern
Cover design, p. 1, pull-out map cover: Karl Anders – Studio für Brand Profiling, Hamburg; design inside: milchhof:atelier, Berlin; design p. 2/3, Discovery Tours: Susan Chaaban Dipl.-Des. (FH)
Translated from German by Paul Fletcher, Jennifer Walcof Neuheiser and Dr. Suzanne Kirkbright
Editorial office: SAW Communications, Redaktionsbüro Dr. Sabine A. Werner, Mainz: Frauke Feuchter, Julia Gilcher, Kristin Smolinna, Dr. Sabine A. Werner; prepress: SAW Communications, Mainz, in cooperation with alles mit Medien, Mainz
Useful phrases: Martina Miethig and Mai Van Danh

MIX
Paper from
responsible sources
FSC® C124385

DOS & DON'TS 👆

A few things to bear in mind in Vietnam

DO AVOID TRAVELLING AT THE TIME OF THE TET FESTIVAL

At Tet, the Vietnamese New Year, the whole of Vietnam and millions of ex-patriate Vietnamese are on the move. Tours and tickets – if any are available – can be up to 50 percent more expensive. Rooms suddenly cost double the normal rate, public services and tours are paralysed for a week and many restaurants and shops close.

DON'T GIVE TO BEGGARS

Even if they arouse your compassion, do not give money to street beggars. In the country there are thousands of professional beggars exploited by unscrupulous racketeers. Instead, donate your money to one of the charitable organisations that cares for street children and the disabled, such as *Saigon Children (www.saigonchildren.com)*, *Reaching Out (www.reachingoutvietnam.com)* in Hoi An or the *Hoa Sua School (www.hoasuaschool.edu.vn)* in Hanoi. For more information, visit *Terre des Hommes (www.terredeshommes.org)*.

DON'T RIDE A MOTORCYCLE WITHOUT A HELMET

The law requires a helmet to be worn when riding motorcycles. If you plan to take a motorcycle tour or travel frequently with a moped taxi, your best bet is to bring a good (integral) helmet from home with you! Vietnam may have the world's highest death rate for traffic accidents, but the Vietnamese helmets tend to be stylish accessories, i.e. military or "Hello Kitty" helmets, that provide little protection.

DON'T PAY TOO MUCH

When paying for a taxi or cyclo or at the ticket counter for the citadel in Hue or buying fruit on the street, make sure to keep a good eye on the value of the banknote that you've handed over – otherwise you risk the rather common problem that the seller will claim to have received a 10,000 dong note instead of a 100,000 dong note. Make sure to be just as careful in checking the change that you get back!

DON'T VISIT NATIONAL PARKS AT THE WEEKEND

You cannot expect to hear nothing but the birds in the national parks at the weekends because the trails and the local accommodation options are often overrun with troops of Vietnamese with lots of beer and loud music. As a general rule, avoid spending the night in the parks at the weekend or on holidays if at all possible.

DON'T TOUCH THE MONKS

Orthodox Buddhists abide strictly by the rule that no woman may touch them. If this happens to a monk, he has to carry out time-consuming cleansing rituals. If you would like to present a gift to a monk, the best way to do this is via a tour guide, for example. Also, wait to be offered a hand to shake – if a monk does not offer you his hand, do not under any circumstances take the initiative.